More Praise for *Make an I*

"This book is a must-read for everyone who is involved in a leadership position at any level in an organization. An excellent 'self-reflection' manual, it was a quick read that kept me engaged! Dr. Pastin's efforts should cause readers to step back and look at the culture of their entity and the moral compass direction they have set for themselves. Its practical application is self-evident."

—**Michael H. Covert, FACHE, President and CEO, Palomar Health, San Diego, California**

"Look no further if you are truly interested in finding practical solutions for difficult and complex ethical problems affecting you within your organization! Dr. Mark Pastin has provided an easy-to-follow, practical approach to effectively deal with today's intricate, complex, and at times dilemmatic ethical situations. Speaking from decades of world-class academic and consultancy experience in ethics, his narrative style keeps your interests going and makes the reading seem more like a novel rather than a heavy-duty academic work."

—**Constant Cheng, Professor, George Mason University**

"Dr. Pastin elegantly discusses modern ethics with a unique perspective that engages the reader with humor and real-life applicability. This is an exceptional exploration of ethical challenges faced in business along with a set of effective tools for overcoming them. A must-read for individuals looking to successfully navigate corporate America with integrity."

—**Debra Burock, PhD, CCP, Regional Director of Program Evaluation and Practice Development, NHS Human Services**

"*Make an Ethical Difference* delivers a clear and direct message: merely talking about honesty and integrity is not enough. Every one of us routinely faces ethical challenges, whether we recognize them as such or not. Dr. Pastin calls on his forty years of experience as an ethics advisor in this thought-provoking book that provides user-friendly, common-sense tools that have been tested and proven in many challenging situations. It is an invaluable guide to the leader who wants to make a lasting difference!"

—**James Neal, Chief Compliance Officer, Millennium Laboratories**

"*Make an Ethical Difference* is an informative and enjoyable read! I will definitely be utilizing the principles/tools that were so thoroughly and creatively explained. The case scenarios were most appreciated as they provided realistic examples that anyone can relate to."

—**Amber King, Chief Human Resource Officer/Chief Compliance Officer, NorthCrest Medical Center**

"Mark Pastin's book gives a variety of stimulating situational examples of some of the ethical issues that he has personally encountered in his international consulting work. He does not just point out the problem but gives a range of workable tools for everyday consideration as we all run into ethnically challenging situations. As a result of using these tools, we all might be better off as we develop our own ethics eye/ethics sense."

—**Daniel C. Brenenstuhl, Managing Director, International Business Seminars**

"One quote from Mark Pastin's book rings true for all of us: 'The problem in getting ethical conduct to surface in organizations is that people lack the confidence that if they do the right thing, they will succeed.' With case studies and a solid easy-to-read style, Mark gives you the tools and confidence to ingrain ethical conduct in your organization. I highly recommend this book for any C-suite executive."

—**Lâle White, CEO and Chairman, XIFIN, Inc.**

Make an Ethical Difference

Make an Ethical Difference

Tools for Better Action

Mark Pastin

BK

Berrett–Koehler Publishers, Inc.
San Francisco
a BK Business book

Berrett-Koehler Publishers, Inc.
235 Montgomery Street, Suite 650
San Francisco, CA 94104-2916
Tel: (415) 288-0260   Fax: (415) 362-2512   www.bkconnection.com

Ordering Information

Quantity sales. Special discounts are available on quantity purchases by corporations, associations, and others. For details, contact the "Special Sales Department" at the Berrett-Koehler address above.

Individual sales. Berrett-Koehler publications are available through most bookstores. They can also be ordered directly from Berrett-Koehler: Tel: (800) 929-2929; Fax: (802) 864-7626; www.bkconnection.com

Orders for college textbook/course adoption use. Please contact Berrett-Koehler: Tel: (800) 929-2929; Fax: (802) 864-7626.

Orders by U.S. trade bookstores and wholesalers. Please contact Ingram Publisher Services, Tel: (800) 509-4887; Fax: (800) 838-1149; E-mail: customer.service@ingrampublisherservices.com; or visit www.ingrampublisherservices.com/Ordering for details about electronic ordering.

Berrett-Koehler and the BK logo are registered trademarks of Berrett-Koehler Publishers, Inc.

Printed in the United States of America

Berrett-Koehler books are printed on long-lasting acid-free paper. When it is available, we choose paper that has been manufactured by environmentally responsible processes. These may include using trees grown in sustainable forests, incorporating recycled paper, minimizing chlorine in bleaching, or recycling the energy produced at the paper mill.

Library of Congress Cataloging-in-Publication Data

Pastin, Mark, 1944-
    Make an ethical difference : tools for better action / Mark Pastin, CEO, Council of
    Ethical Organizations. -- First edition.
        pages cm
    Includes index.
    ISBN 978-1-60994-911-2 (pbk.)
    1. Business ethics. 2. Leadership--Moral and ethical aspects. 3. Ethics.
    4. Organizational behavior. I. Title.
    HF5387.P373 2013
    174'.4--dc23
                                                                    2013031986

First Edition
18 17 16 15 14 13   10 9 8 7 6 5 4 3 2 1

Interior design and production by Dovetail Publishing Services
Cover design by Richard Adelson

To Christina

for her love, belief, and patience

*"When the rain falls, it falls on guilty
and innocent alike."*

—Matthew 5:45

Contents

Preface

I don't like ethics books. I find them boring, sometimes smug, and mostly uninstructive. I have earned a living giving ethical advice for 40 years and I have never once found myself reaching for an ethics book to help solve a problem. None of the many ethics books I have read are worth much when you are faced with a problem that needs to be solved in a given time and within fixed resources. That sort of problem doesn't even come up in most ethics books.

Why, then, write an ethics book?

Because all the bad ethics books can't hide the fact that many of us would like to do something about the ethical problems that surround us. And there is something we can do.

I have faith that people want to live in a world in which doing the right thing is a more common occurrence—even an expectation. In working with organizations, large and small, I have seen this desire to do right in virtually every one of them, even those that have made critical ethical blunders. Despite this desire, neither our organizations nor our society are getting more ethical. In fact, there is a sense that ethics is spiraling downward. If I don't expect you to treat me honestly, I act defensively toward you—which in turn gives you less reason to trust me. Before long, we're suing each other.

There is a disconnect between what we want for our organizations and our society and the reality being created by our actions.

In my work as an ethics consultant, my job is to reconnect the wishes and desires of the ethical individuals in an organization with the actions of the organization itself. It is possible to do this and, more importantly, it is possible to learn how to do this. I am not suggesting that it is easy or that success is always achieved. However, over time I have found tools that help reconnect the ethical desires of individuals with the reality of organizations. These tools are the backbone of *Make an Ethical Difference*.

One of the problems in getting ethical conduct to surface in organizations is that people lack confidence that if they do the right thing, they will succeed. If you have no confidence that you will succeed, you have planted the seeds of failure.

A second problem is that we spend billions of dollars trying to gain business skills in leadership, effectiveness, strategic planning, diversity, quality improvement—you name it and there is a program for it. But when we set out to accomplish something ethically, we approach the situation without thought of training or tools. If it can take years to learn how to be a leader in a three-person work group, why do we suppose that we either know how to get ethical results or we don't? Why assume there is nothing to learn?

It is especially frustrating that millions of people are required to undergo something called "ethics training," which is really just about following the company's rules—or else. I wish that some of this time were used to talk about how to make our organizations better. In fact, one of the goals of *Make an Ethical Difference* is that people use it to add some oomph to these training sessions. There is nothing wrong with following company rules, but there is more to the story.

I wrote this book for people who want to do the right thing, who want to have justified confidence in their ethical beliefs, and who are willing to learn how to help connect their ethical wishes with the actions of the groups and organizations to which they belong.

Make an Ethical Difference is a book for doers—for individuals who want to make an ethical difference through their daily actions. You do not have to buy into an ideology to benefit from this book nor do you have to share the author's beliefs about any controversial ethical issue. You just need to trust your ethics sense, be willing to sharpen it, and have the boldness to act on it.

So, unlike the ethics books that I don't like, the success or failure of *Make an Ethical Difference* is in actions as opposed to opinions. If you disagree with everything I say here but still become more capable of ethical action, I will count that as success.

If you want to measure your own success in creating an ethical workplace, you may wish to employ a survey tool called "My Ethical Workplace," described at the back of this book. This tool not only allows you to assess how ethical your workplace currently is, it also allows you to measure your success in influencing that workplace for the better.

A number of cases are discussed in *Make an Ethical Difference*. Each of them incorporates a situation within my direct experience, unless otherwise noted. However, there is no point in trying to guess the companies and other organizations involved, since names and other nonessential facts have been changed in most cases.

I never expected to make a living as an ethics advisor. I owe those who have hired me, valued my advice, and sometimes followed it. It is this work that allowed me to develop the tools included here. I have also benefited from opportunities to speak on these topics and learn from the people I met doing this. While I know that what is written here is not the final word on any part of ethics, every idea and tool has been tested in challenging, real-world circumstances.

Just as I do not like ethics books, publishers do not like them either. Ethics books continue to be published because there is an obvious public interest in ethics. But for the most part ethics books do not succeed, as they wander off into the land of the hypothetical. Given the bad reputation of ethics books, I am very grateful to the unbelievably dedicated Berrett-Koehler team, and especially to my editor, Steve Piersanti, for his commitment to this book. Steve gave me the encouragement I needed when I told him I wanted to write a book about ethical change. It would be unforgivable not to acknowledge the nearly daily support of Jeevan Sivasubramaniam. Being an author is often ego deflating, and Jeevan kept me glued together when I needed it.

Too many people have shaped my thinking to acknowledge them properly here. I had the good fortune to study with the two great ethicists of the twentieth century, Roderick Firth and John Rawls. While neither understood my desire to "get my hands dirty" in the business world, they empowered me to do so. I have learned so much from my colleagues at the Council of Ethical Organizations. My wife, Christina Brecto, has read every word of this book (several times) and anticipated the views of the editors at every turn. It helps to have an in-house editor.

Introduction

Better Action

> *"How selfish soever man shall be supposed, there are evidently some principles in his nature, which interest him in the fortune of others, and render their happiness necessary to him, though he derives nothing from it except the pleasure of seeing it."*
>
> —Adam Smith, 1759

Somewhere in corporate America, a discussion like this is occurring.

SITUATION #1 *Less Is More*

Ever since the upstart Greek yogurt companies Chobani and Fage came along, the big dogs in the yogurt industry have been hurting. For years, profits soared as they sold smaller and smaller containers of yogurt at ever higher prices. As soon as one company reduced the size of its yogurt containers, the other companies followed suit. As a bonus, they could claim to have reduced the number of calories per unit of their product, which was accomplished by making the portions smaller.

1

Today, one of the old-line yogurt companies is considering challenging the upstarts by introducing its own Greek yogurt at a lower price and with fewer calories. The trick is to fool consumers into thinking that its product is less expensive and less fattening simply by giving them less product per container. It worked before, so why not again? But someone in the room asks, "Is it right to compete by fooling our customers?" To which another person responds, "We never tricked anyone. We simply helped our customers do something they should do in any case, which is to control portion size."

Whether it is yogurt or another product, discussions of this kind occur in business every day. Formulate the advice you would give to the old-line yogurt company. At the end of this chapter, you can compare your advice to the advice actually given. The tools introduced throughout this book will help you find the right path in just such situations.

Make an Ethical Difference is about having confidence that we can make sound ethical decisions—and that we can act on them. And it is about making ethical actions effective in the groups and organizations in which we participate.

When it comes to today's ethical problems, it is up to us to do something about them. We do not trust our political, economic, religious, and social institutions to meet today's ethical challenges. These institutions have served us for years, and they often served us well. As much as this is true, we sense that these institutions are not up to today's ethical challenges. Just as a virus can evolve more rapidly than our immune systems, many of our problems, particularly those involving ethics, have evolved beyond the reach of our institutions. If our institutions cannot meet today's ethical challenges, it is time for us to act as ethically concerned individuals and groups.

Many ethics books invite you to agree or disagree with the author, who is pretty sure about what other people should believe and do. This is not such a book. To benefit from *Make an Ethical Difference* you need not agree with me about any issue of public controversy. This book is about *how* to make ethical decisions and act on them. I am not going to tell you which decisions to make or how I, or anyone else, expect you to act.

Make an Ethical Difference is partly based on my experience as an ethics advisor to hundreds of organizations of every kind and size—and in some of the worst ethical situations of our time. From this experience, I have learned a lot about why people make poor ethical choices and how to stop this from happening. I have also learned the value of action over opinion. One thing that gives ethics a bad name is that ethical issues never seem to be resolved. Ethics often seems to be oriented more toward critiquing what has happened than toward influencing what *will* happen. In *Make an Ethical Difference,* our view is firmly forward on the future we can create through ethical action.

Your Ethics Sense

Make an Ethical Difference is built on a radical theme, which is that *individuals have an innate ability to see what is right and do it.* I sometimes call this innate ability to see what is right "the ethics eye," and this book will help you recognize this ability in yourself. Once you acknowledge your native ability to see what is right, it is comparatively easy to sharpen this ability. Trusting your ability to see what is right will give you the confidence to take actions that make an ethical difference.

A basic question is, "If I have this innate ethics sense, why don't other people agree with me?" In fact, if we have this innate ability, why are there broad, fight-to-the-death disagreements among religions, political ideologies, and whole societies about right and wrong?

It may seem like this is the knockout punch for the whole idea of an innate ethics sense, but it isn't. The kinds of disagreements cited above exist in all branches of knowledge, including those based on the evidence of the five recognized senses. There are exactly analogous disagreements in physics, psychology, mathematics, and aesthetics. Would anyone argue that we cannot do physics because there are endless arguments about the basic components of matter?

Deep, recalcitrant disagreements are common to such fields as physics and astronomy. The disagreement between Copernicus and Ptolemy about the position of the Earth in the Universe was profound and not easily resolved. Because both viewpoints made the same predictions about the then observable movements of the planets, the eye—visible observation—seemed unable to decide between the theories. This disagreement did not lead us to distrust the human eye. Eventually, that self-same human eye was able, *with the use of more powerful instruments,* to decisively support the Copernican viewpoint. In the same way, the tools provided in *Make an Ethical Difference* are designed to sharpen your ethics sense. They are instruments for sharpening your vision of right and wrong.

Some would point out that at least some scientific disputes are eventually settled—and in ethics nothing ever seems to get settled. But one of the reasons that some scientific disputes are settled is that we are willing to count them as settled. Some people still believe in astrology, which is a version of Ptolemaic astronomy. This does not lead us to conclude that the Earth might really be at the center of the Universe. In physics, there is dispute over whether the basic components of reality are waves or particles or strings or something else for that matter. We do not conclude that we will never settle anything in physics.

It is a theme of *Make an Ethical Difference* that *the fact that people disagree about ethics does not show that we lack an ethics sense. It shows that ethical issues are as complex as the problems in other branches of knowledge.* Once we understand the causes of ethical disagreements, we will be better able to settle them.

Tools for Better Action

One reason for today's pessimism about ethics is that a decline in ethical expectations is a self-reinforcing, downward spiral. The lower my expectations of ethical conduct from others, the less likely I am to enter into relationships with them based on honesty and trust. Instead of shaking hands over a simple transaction, I will "lawyer up." Others, in turn, have less reason to be honest with me and trust me, since my behavior toward them is cagey and untrusting. This downward spiral of expectations can only be reversed through focused action to break the cycle. *Make an Ethical Difference* is about just such action.

In order to take action to stop the downward ethics spiral, we need tools to sharpen our ethics sense. *It is possible to learn to be an effective ethics change agent through the use of proven tools.* These tools have been developed over a forty-year period and have been tested in many challenging situations. To build confidence in these tools, we apply them to situations in which an ethical action is required.

I believe that individuals can take constructive action on ethical issues. Sometimes it seems that issues are called "ethical" just to put them in a locked box labeled "insoluble." This is a self-defeating way to think about ethics because it blocks all possible action. If you wonder where this kind of thinking leads, just take a look around. On the other hand, if you want to stop wringing your hands about ethical decline and do something about it, we have a journey together.

SITUATION #1   *Less Is More (continued)*

Here is the advice I gave to the old-line yogurt company.

"You got into this predicament by using trickery to increase profits—and it worked for quite a while. However, you also made yourself vulnerable to the upstart Greek yogurt companies and now you are paying the price. Even if you challenge the upstarts with more of the same trickery, there is no guarantee that you will succeed. Now that you have feisty competitors, they may reveal your strategy for what it is. You should at least match the quality and portions of the upstarts while working hard to out-market them. You are still the familiar brand and you have enormous advantages in commanding shelf space. This is the ethical way to compete, and it will also ensure that any customers you regain will stay loyal to you."

As we gather tools in the coming pages, you will be able to see why I gave this advice and decide whether or not you agree with it.

Chapter One

Know the Rules before You Play

*"The master knows the rules without suffering them,
the slave suffers the rules without knowing them."*

—Chinese proverb

SITUATION #2 *This Land Is Your Land*

I once consulted to a company in the "raw land" business. Land is considered "raw" if it is either not currently in use or is used only for farming and has no roads or utilities. Buying such land is highly speculative, because developing the land for residential or commercial use depends on approvals at many levels of government, not to mention someone willing to pay for the roads and other infrastructure. My client had a buyer for a large chunk of raw land, a huge public company whose bonds were rated AAA. When it came down to negotiations, the public company offered a reasonable price, but offered to double the price if my client would accept its AAA rated bonds instead of cash. When the public company's chief financial officer computed the

9

value of the bonds on offer to my client, he made a huge error in my client's favor. The only condition the public company put on its offer was that my client decide then and there. My client asked me, "Should I take the cash now or go for the much higher valued bonds?"

How would you advise the client? In formulating this advice, use the ethical decision-making tool that focuses this chapter.

I have spent 40 years as an ethics advisor to organizations of all kinds, ranging from global multinationals to small start-ups. Needless to say, this was not a clever career plan nurtured in my youth. Ethical situations just seemed to find me. In many of these situations, an ethical change was necessary for the survival of an organization. This was often because the organization had been caught doing something unethical, and often illegal as well. I have not always been able to effect the needed change, but over time I have gotten better at it. I have developed tools for ethical change that increase the chance of a positive outcome.

This book distills the lessons learned in hundreds of situations into a practical guide—a set of tools—to use for ethical action and change. In this chapter, we introduce the first of these tools.

The tools provided here can be used to solve ethical problems as well as problems well beyond the domain of ethics. The ways of thinking that encourage ethical action are essential to the sustained success of groups and organizations, whether or not there is an ethical issue. In fact, I have learned that those who can see the difference between right and wrong—and act on what they see—often have other attributes that contribute to their success.

The world will not be free of ethical defect as a result of what is written here. Nor do I pretend to have surpassed the wisdom of the ages in terms of philosophical ethics. Fortunately, you do not have to be a sage to make a positive difference in ethics. *Each and every one of us has the experience of doing something right or making something better.* Each of us has an innate ability to contribute to ethics, and my goal is to help you find that ability in yourself, trust it, act on it, and make an ethical difference.

Beyond Ideology

A person can *learn* how to make a constructive ethical difference in the groups and organizations to which they belong. If you doubt that this is true, it may be because theologians, philosophers, and psychologists have often mystified ethics to make us think that ethical betterment depends on accepting their views. Those who say you cannot change ethics outside of their favored ideology or discipline do a disservice to ethics, and to people. They are using our desire for ethical betterment to promote the viewpoint they favor.

These same ideologues have been trying to convince us for centuries that ethical disputes are too difficult for us to resolve on our own. We are supposed to believe that the best we can do is to demur to the "great minds" and not ask too many hard questions. But these great minds, despite centuries of effort, have not resolved many ethical issues. And where is it proven that, despite confusions and disagreements, we do not have an innate ability to find the right path? Where has it been proven that we need an ideology to guide us?

We see later that the whole idea of an ethics ideology is ill conceived. While you can and will arrive at ethical opinions and generalizations, they will be built upon your ethics sense—and not upon the dictates of an authority.

ETHICAL CHANGE

If we are going to create ethical change, the first question we need to ask is, "What is it that we are trying to change?"

Interlude: What Ethics Is—And What It Isn't

When we think about living in a world where the unethical often succeed, it is common to bemoan the loss of an inner ethical compass, a personal integrity, which is somehow no longer getting installed in folks. This, of course, assumes that you and I have this inner compass and that we recognize its absence in others. When you live in the middle of ethical disputes, you quickly learn that all parties to the dispute have this "I have it; you don't" belief about an inner ethical compass. In fact, as you read this, you are probably pretty sure that you have this inner compass and wonder if the author of this book has any ethics. Who is the author to tell me anything about ethics at all? In other words, you have it, and maybe I don't. I have never yet met a person who told me (except with tongue in cheek) that he or she was below average in ethics or completely without ethics.

The only way to break out of the I-have-it-and-you-don't circle is to understand what ethics is. I emphasize that knowing what ethics is is *not* the same as knowing what *good ethics* is. Ethics is our *topic,* and we need to understand the topic before we sort out good ethics from bad ethics, right from wrong. And it will help us figure out why it seems that each of us thinks we have ethics while others may not.

All sorts of entities can be said to have (or lack) ethics: people, companies, agencies, even countries. Start with people.

A person's ethics is no more or less than the set of principles that the person will not breach, except under extreme duress. (A parent who is ordinarily truthful may lie to save their child's life. Truthfulness is still part of the parent's ethics but the duress is extreme.) If you want to know about my ethics, you want to know what you can expect of me in various situations. If you lend me money, can you trust me to repay it even if it is difficult for me to do so? If you leave your kids with me, can you trust me to treat your kids as well as my own? If you share information with me at work, will I use it to make myself look smarter than you? The answers to these questions will tell you a lot about my ethics. We can summarize this by saying that a person's ethics consists of the *ground rules,* which determine what that person will and will not do. These are the principles that guide a person's actions except when the person is under extreme duress, such as when the survival of the person or a member of their family is perceived to be threatened.

13

A person's ethics is somewhat like a computer's operating system. The operating system does not do many tasks itself, but it determines what tasks a computer can and cannot do. When you use a computer, you usually don't notice the operating system. But if the computer constantly locks up, it is time to look at the operating system.

In the classic cult movie *Repo Man,* actor Harry Dean Stanton plays "Bud," an elder statesman of repo men, people who repossess cars when the owners miss payments. Bud takes an apprentice, Otto, played by Emilio Estevez, under his wing. At one point Bud admonishes Otto to honor the "repo man code of ethics." Even though this is played for laughs, it makes sense. You can imagine the repo man code of ethics including such pearls as, "Avoid situations in which your actions are likely to provoke violence" and "Take only what you are authorized to repossess." Even endeavors as ugly as repossession have ground rules.

A corollary of seeing ethics as ground rules is that what a person *says* about ethics may have little to do with his or her actual ethics. Everyone knows what they are expected to say about ethics. If I tell my new neighbor that I am not interested in him as a person and that I am interested only in the tools I can borrow from him, that neighbor will not be my friend. If I tell my co-workers that I am only interested in looking better than they do to the boss, they will keep their distance. You have to choose your ethical words carefully. I should say to my neighbor, "If you need anything, just ask." I should say to my co-workers, "I always take a

win-win approach with my colleagues." I may not expect to
be believed when I say these things since I am just saying
what is expected. But I will at least show that I know what is
expected.

Another corollary of defining ethics as ground rules
is that a person's ethics, their ground rules, are normally
stable. These are the rules that determine everything else the
person may or may not do, but these rules are themselves
seldom subject to change. Even when we are not aware of
ground rules, they guide our judgments of right and wrong,
better and worse. That is not to say that ground rules cannot
change, or even that it takes a big effort to change them; it is
just that in the ordinary course of events, a person's ground
rules are stable and unquestioned.

Even though ethics is not normally defined as ground
rules, I believe this is what we mean when we talk about ethics. When I want to know about someone's ethics, I am trying
to predict what they will do in certain situations. Knowing
their ground rules helps me do that.

Organizations and groups have ethics too—some good
and some not so good. Just as with people, an organization's
ground rules help us predict how it will act. We often think
of the ground rules of organizations that have failed in one
way or another. For example, it is hard to think about the Gulf
oil spill and not conclude that British Petroleum was "talking
green" while operating on the ground rule, "If something
goes wrong, blame someone—anyone—else." But there
are also positive examples of organizational ground rules.

Nordstrom has built an empire by acting on the ground rule, "Treat a customer returning a pair of shoes just like a customer buying one." Just as with individuals, organizational ground rules tend to be stable and unquestioned.

If we see ethics as ground rules, ethics are not so mysterious. Different theories about ethics can make ethics seem mysterious, but it all comes down to what people will and will not do. That is what we are interested in. Once you realize this, you can quit worrying about ethics as some sort of mental state, brain wave, or mystical experience. These things may influence your ethics, but they are not your ethics. Even if you achieve some sort of beatific mental state, when you cheat me on a contract, you are a cheater. On the other hand, if you are impeccably honest in dealing with me, I couldn't care less about your brain waves.

When we say that many folks no longer seem to have an inner ethical compass, we are saying that we cannot rely on their ground rules to ensure truthfulness, honesty, and concern for others. It is a mistake to rely on their ground rules in personal or business relationships. Because ground rules help make actions predictable, we do not find much predictability in dealing with one another. For this reason, we try, mostly without success, to restore predictability through a landslide of laws, regulations, and complex contracts. This is not a revelation; it is the defining mark of a world with ethics in decline.

There are other ethical words that we have to understand to pursue ethical change. These include morality, integrity, and character. These words are easier to understand in terms of ground rules. For example, we can now see that a person's integrity consists of acting in accordance with his or her own ground rules. Thus, even a person whose ground rules are questionable can have integrity in living up to those ground rules. Character has several meanings but one of them is that a person has character if they follow their ground rules even when it is extremely difficult to do so. Morality is a matter of having ground rules, specifically, ground rules that match what we consider to be right and wrong from the perspective of our own ground rules.

Once we see ethics as ground rules, being an ethical change agent seems to be no more or less than changing the ground rules of a person, group, or organization. You might think a good behavioral psychologist would be in the best position to help us bring about ethical change by manipulating punishments and rewards. And this, I believe, is what some influential thinkers such as B. F. Skinner, the father of behaviorism, have thought. For them it all comes down to the carrot, the stick— and the ass between them.

This misses this point. While we have a working definition of what ethics is, it does not tell us what *good* ethics is or what *bad* ethics is. Even if the carrot-and-stick approach worked, it would not give us the faintest idea of which ethical changes to pursue. Another way of putting this is to say that not all ethical change is good. Indeed, one of the things that motivates us to pursue ethical change is the sense that there has already been ethical change— and not entirely for the better. So our question is, *How do we know which ethical changes to bring about?* What actions will allow us to make an ethical difference in a positive sense?

EASY TO SEE: HARD TO DO

While it may seem impossibly hard to figure out just what ethical changes are for the better, this is often not the case. When an organization asks me for ethical advice, I am not there to make things worse. And it is seldom hard to tell what would be better. An example:

SITUATION #3 *Outside Looking In*

The board of directors of one of the world's largest financial services companies hired several consultants to help with an ethical issue. The issue turned out to be in the executive suite, and to some extent in the bedrooms of those in the executive suite. The CEO of the company had put a lot of trust in a younger employee with whom he was having an affair. Unfortunately, the younger employee abused this trust in a way that might soon become public. Or so the board feared. The board brought in the outsiders, including me, to "gain perspective" and "contain" the problem. While the board knew that it would have to make changes in the executive team, it also knew that the story would be a juicy one in the media. The board asked, "What will our employees think once they see what their leaders have been up to?"

The consultants' task was not to undo the wrongdoing. Too late for that. Our job was to keep the rot from spreading from the top down throughout the organization, thereby creating even more ethical problems. When the employees of an organization learn that the CEO made huge business blunders on the advice of his lover, they often conclude that the whole company is corrupt and lower their own expectations of ethical conduct.

It came down to this. When executives set a bad example, the ground rules of an otherwise decent organization may shift. Employees may feel betrayed in their commitment to doing the right thing when the folks at the top clearly aren't. This organization was a basically honest company. So the task was to keep the ground rules from slipping as a result of the soon-to-be-disclosed scandal. Doing this was a matter of some complexity, since you can't just say, "Your CEO is a bum but we don't want you to be bums." It was important not to compound the internal damage to the company by trying to convince the employees that what they would inevitably hear was not true. You can destroy the integrity of an organization by lying about the wrongdoing of its leadership. It's the old adage about the cover-up being worse than what is being covered up. So the problem was how to communicate with employees in a manner that neither hid the truth nor demoralized the company.

The consultants recommended that the board clean house in the executive suite in as short a time as feasible without leaving the company rudderless. Almost everyone in the executive suite had some inkling of what was going on and either aided and abetted it, or at least tolerated it. In this way, if the issue did become public, the company would already have taken action. Employees would see that the improper conduct was handled decisively and that the board would be viewed as taking strong action to protect the reputation of the company.

The board initially rejected this advice instead trying to salvage more of the company's leadership team. The CEO got wind of the advice given to the board and had the consultants fired. (It is the job of an ethics consultant to be fired in such situations if it helps the company move ahead.) When the board saw that the CEO was not taking decisive action, they accepted the consultants' advice. When the story became public, it was not exciting news since the main actors were long gone.

Even though *fixing* what was wrong was not easy, it was not hard to *know* what needed to be fixed. It took no genius to see that communicating to employees that ethical expectations were still high, despite the actions of some executives, was the right thing to do. These employees handled the personal finances of tens of thousands of members of the public, who deserved honest treatment. Philosophical arguments about right and wrong did not come into play. In this case it was easy to *see* what needed to be done. And this case is not the exception; it is the rule. A premise of *Make an Ethical Difference* is that there is a sense that allows us to see what is right, even if we sometimes put a stick in its eye.

Understanding ethics as ground rules also provides us with our first tool for making ethical decisions.

TOOL #1 *Read the Ground Rules*

When a situation presents an ethical issue, *look beyond the individuals and their actions and uncover the ground rules that help explain their actions.* Remember that ground rules are rules that will only be breached *under extreme duress.* This means that you should pay particular attention to situations in which the individuals had to make hard choices. For example, while everyone says that they are loyal to their friends, have these individuals demonstrated loyalty when it was not easy to do so? While everyone talks about trust, have there been situations in which these individuals acted on trust instead of holding out for a signed contract? Think about what you know of the individuals in terms of the choices they have made.

If the situation involves groups or organizations as well as individuals, do the same thing for each group or organization. Look beyond the public statements of values and principles and *read the actual ground rules.* Most companies say that their employees are the key to their success. But when the analysts start biting their nails, many of these companies are quick to start firing people. This would not be their first response if the company's ground rules required that it be as loyal to its employees as it expects it employees to be to it.

Write out the ground rules of the affected parties as specifically as possible. Being specific about the ground rules allows you to communicate with those affected by the situation in terms that will resonate with them. Rather than working with generalizations that don't tell you much in the situation, drill down to the ground rules actually at issue. It is far more useful to know that someone acts on the ground rule "Put shareholder value above all other interests" than it is to know that the individual acts on the ground rule "Act in the interests of shareholders." Someone acting on the former ground rule may act ruthlessly in situations in which shareholder value is threatened. A person with the latter ground rule may allow other priorities to affect their choices. If the ground rules you have written down are not helping you understand a situation, get more specific. Until you write the ground rules down, you are likely to stick with generalities that will not help unravel the situation.

You know you have the ground rules right when you can predict what the parties to a situation will or will not do next. Remember that the organization or organizations involved in the situation have ground rules too. For example, in the situation involving the financial services company, the ground rule at issue was whether executives were held to the same standards of conduct as other employees. Written down it is clearer: "When an employee engages in wrongdoing, the discipline of that employee is consistent regardless of the rank or function of the employee." This ground rule is important to any organization that acts ethically while achieving consistent performance.

Remember the analogy between ground rules and the operating system of a computer. If you were trying to understand something the computer was doing, it would not be that helpful to know the general principle, "Computers run on a series of '0's and '1's." But it might be useful to know the more specific, "The computer is running on Operating System 10.6.8."

Thinking in terms of ground rules may seem like such a simple concept that it can hardly be an important tool for ethical change. But by viewing situations in terms of ground rules, you can not only better understand why certain things happen, you can also understand *what you have to change*—the ground rules—to be a successful ethical change agent. Instead of just being puzzled by the wrongdoing we observe, we can focus instead on what the wrongdoing means in terms of grounds rules—ground rules that we may need to change.

Reading the ground rules is particularly useful for figuring out why organizations do things. While at least some people are reflective, organizations typically are not. Yes, they have retreats and the like, but these are more about rearranging the furniture than redesigning the space in which the furniture goes. Listening to what organizations say will not help nearly as much as observing the limits of their conduct in terms of ground rules.

When people do think about the ground rules of organizations, they often talk about the "culture" of an organization. When "culture" is used in this way, it is a metaphor suggesting that unseen factors drive organizational behavior. But it is not a great metaphor as the word "culture" also suggests things that can only be changed over a long period of time. And this is not always true with respect to an organization's ground rules. If the executives in the above financial services case had gotten away with their misconduct, the ground rules of the organization would have shifted—for the worse—almost immediately. That is why I prefer the analogy between ground rules and operating systems better than the analogy with culture. If you change one thing in a computer's operating system, there may be widespread ramifications. Ethics is like that, too.

SITUATION #2 *This Land Is Your Land (continued)*

In the situation at the beginning of the chapter, I advised my client to take cash. I asked myself, "If the public corporation's AAA bond rating is justified, what ground rule is the corporation following in offering my client so much more in terms of bonds?" If you cannot find a ground rule explaining an action, that is a sign that there is more to a situation than meets the eye. In Chapter Two, we learn that it is also essential to look at the interests in a situation. Absent a plausible ground rule, I assumed the corporation was acting on its own interests. Another ethics warning sign was that the public corporation was putting extreme pressure on my client to decide on the spot. They didn't want the client to think the situation over and take a closer look at the public company's finances. The public company was American Continental, a company whose imminent demise triggered the implosion of the real estate and saving and loans industries in the United States. Cash looked pretty good after all.

Chapter Two

Navigating the Minefield of Interests

"Self-interest speaks all sorts of tongues, and plays all sorts of roles, even that of disinterestedness."

—Francois duc de la Rochefoucauld

When you work as an ethics advisor, you bump into smelly situations. You see organizations trying to hide ethical failures and leaders trying to escape blame. But, even in these situations, there is something to learn. One of the first things you learn is that the truth told about ethical situations is seldom the whole truth or even part of the truth. You are dealing with *images* of the truth formed by those with an interest in making the situation appear a certain way. In many cases, the interests trying to enforce their image of the ethical truth are powerful. *You need to recognize the interests involved in an ethical situation and know how to navigate them.* And so, when I am called on as an ethics advisor, one of my first questions is, "Whose interests are involved—and what are those interests?"

Ethics and Interests

In order to understand ethics and interests, we need to put some myths about interests behind us. This also enables us to introduce two tools in this chapter for finding the interests and facing the facts in an ethical situation.

Many people believe that ethics and interests don't mix. But ethics does not have a problem with interests. Interests provide the energy of human activity and motivate change, competition and progress. So why do interests have a bad name when it comes to ethics? And why do we have such disparaged categories as "self-interests," "special interests," and "vested interests"?

Interlude: Stakeholders and Interests

Many thinkers, especially in the field of business decision making, are so adverse to discussing interests that they developed a new term for those who have an interest in a situation or decision. They call these interested parties "stakeholders."[1] The term *stakeholder* has become so popular since it was first introduced in the business lexicon over thirty years ago that I would not be surprised to find Lady Gaga calling her fans Little Stakeholders.

In its literal meaning, a stakeholder is the holder of a wager. But the modern use of this term is a pun on the term *shareholder*. It is meant to suggest that the leaders of corporations should not only manage in the interests of shareholders, who pay the managers to do just that, but also in the interests of a wide variety of private and public interest groups. Calling these groups stakeholders is a verbal manipulation to give them a status equal or comparable to that of shareholders, a status they wouldn't have if we called them what they are—interest groups.

If the point of this stakeholder talk is that managers will not be successful if they spend all of their time thinking about shareholder value, this is stating the obvious. But a corporation is not a public interest group. A corporation is an entity that exists by way of a promise, and that promise is that if the shareholders give the corporation their money, leadership of the corporation will put shareholder value at the top of their priorities. This is not to say that shareholders are the only priority, but they have paid to be at the front of the line.

So rather than dressing up interest groups in the word "stakeholder," we will just call them what they are here, interest groups. It is one of the themes of *Make an Ethical Difference* that managers will only make sound ethical decisions if they are aware of the interests affected by their decisions. But let's not pretend that being an interest group is a bad thing.

One reason interests have a bad name in ethics is that interests often conflict in ways that lead to a lot of ethics name-calling. My interest in hearing loud music while I wash the car may interfere with your interest in taking a nap. "I have a *right* to play music as loudly as I want in my own driveway" versus "I have a *right* to peace and quiet in my own home." Rules are supposed to balance conflicting interests in a way that we can each accept. These rules come in many forms, ranging from rules of etiquette ("Respect your neighbor's wishes") and black-letter rules (noise control laws) to the less visible ground rules that constitute ethics. Of course, not every interest-based conflict can be resolved by appealing to rules. And the very rules intended to balance interests may create other conflicts, including conflicts among the rules themselves. Rules can only resolve a conflict of interests if the parties to the conflict agree upon the rules. If this sounds like a short summary of politics today, that is not far from the truth.

Self-interests are among the more disparaged interests. If I do something I want to do, and thereby keep you from doing something you want to do, you might say that I acted in a (typically) self-interested way. But the term "self-interest" stigmatizes beyond saying I got my way at your expense. It connotes a way of acting that undermines the common good. When I describe someone as self-interested, or selfish, I tag him as unworthy of membership in some of the groups to which I belong, such as the neighborhood where I live or the company for which I work. The self-interested will put themselves first irrespective of "our wishes." Of course, excluding someone from certain groups to which I belong may also be a way of advancing my own interests. In other words, when we describe someone as self-interested, we are often doing so to advance our own interests. By calling someone else self-interested, I seize the high ground in terms of pursuing my own interests.

Special interests also attract censure. When someone calls an interest "special," it means that the interest conflicts with other interests regarded by that person as "common" or "public" interests. Common interests are often so vaguely defined that most any interest could be said to conflict, or agree, with them. When a politician or corporate leader proclaims that they are acting in the common interest, the demagoguery light should flash "on." In truth, we often call something a "special" interest mainly to suggest that it ought to take second place to an interest we favor, an interest we then portray as the common good. And, not every special interest is bad. The interests of scientists engaged in earthquake prediction are special, but they are also commendable. And not every common or public interest is good. There was a time when maintaining slavery was the common interest of a large number of individuals.

Vested interests are interests in keeping things the way they are with respect to a group, organization, or society at large. When we call an interest "vested," it suggests that some person or group has an interest in "blocking progress." But "progress" is not an interest neutral word. To me, progress is what advances my interests or at least interests of which I approve. To you, my interest may be an interest in maintaining the status quo. Not all vested interests are bad either. A vested interest in preserving free speech trumps a non-vested interest in advancing censorship.

When we use the terms "self-interest," "special interest," and "vested interest," we usually signal that the interests in question are not our own. And we suggest that they are inferior to our own. This is a matter of pushing and shoving for position, and it has little to do with ethics.

I am not saying all interests are created equal; they are not. But what makes one interest better or worse than another is not whether it is a self or special or vested interest. It is the *object* of the interest that makes the difference. If I have an interest in observing the suffering of others, my interest is not worthy of approval even if it is widely shared. On the other hand, if I have an interest in curing Alzheimer's disease, my interest is commendable even if it is a self-interest (I want to be a famous doctor) or a special interest (I want a research grant for my department). *What matters about an interest is not who has it but where it leads.*

Philosopher and novelist Ayn Rand earned both a dedicated following and considerable scorn for asserting that selfishness—being self-interested—is a virtue. This was always a bit puzzling since Rand's novels feature heroic figures that are individualistic, but hardly selfish. Ms. Rand created a tempest in a teapot. While she talked about self-interest, she also believed that it was in a person's self-interest to be bold, original, generous, kind, noble. She was not talking about hogging the mashed potatoes. If my (self) interest is in creating situations in which individuals and ideas can flourish, it is not surprising that some might think of pursuing *this* self-interest as virtuous. In truth, Ms. Rand attracted attention to herself and her ideas through the dramatic mechanism of calling a person's interest in being an exceptional person a selfish interest. Ms. Rand failed to recognize that what makes an interest virtuous, or not virtuous, is not to whom the interest belongs—oneself or others—but where the interest leads.

CONSTRUCTIVE INTERESTS

I said that when advising on an ethical problem, among the first questions I ask are, "Whose interests are involved?" and "What are those interests?" This usually makes it clearer why there is a problem or disagreement. It may even make it possible to resolve the situation if those interests can be redirected in a positive direction. In fact, we shall soon introduce a tool designed to find ways in which interests can be aligned to achieve an ethical outcome.

Knowing what interests are involved also allows you to get a better view of the facts. If you want to make a sound ethical judgment, you need to know the facts of a situation as opposed to what someone wants you to believe. A perfect example is weather forecasting. Forecasting decent weather does not attract viewers or improve ratings. (The joke is that weather forecasters in Arizona have poor ratings because the forecast never changes.) However, if you portray all of the extreme possibilities, no matter how remote, you turn the weather into news. In order to understand the weather forecast, you have to take account of the fact that there are those who have more of an interest in boosting their ratings than providing accurate information.

Hidden interests can also mean new options. There may be interests favoring an ethical outcome that have not been given a voice. This is a common issue with respect to legislative and regulatory issues, where certain interests dominate the debate while others go unnoticed. Understanding interests not only gives you insight and information, it may give you exactly what you need to reach an ethical outcome.

If finding and navigating interests seems complicated, it usually isn't in practice. Let's see *how finding the interests* helped resolve a difficult and troubling ethical issue.

SITUATION #4 *School's Out*

Every once in a while, there is an outcry over children being sexually abused in private schools. An association of one state's privately owned schools hired me to help them address a situation created by allegations of abuse in several of the schools owned by its members. They were hoping that a code of conduct or a public set of ethical standards might somehow offset the bad publicity. I knew perfectly well that such a group might try to use a little ethics angel dust to brighten their image without addressing the underlying issues. I made it clear to the group that I had no interest in working with them unless they were committed to doing everything possible to address the underlying problem of children being abused.

It was puzzling that most abuse allegations involved private schools. In many ways, a private school has more to lose from an accusation than a public school since a loss of reputation can close a private school. My first thought was that molesters might target private schools as places of employment because their hiring standards are more lax than those of public schools. In fact, most of the private schools did extensive background checks on employees while the public schools sometimes didn't bother. So what was happening?

When the facts in a situation don't add up, this may be because interests are coloring the facts. So I decided to check the facts. I had a team interview a random sample of parents with young children in school, irrespective of whether their kids went to private or public schools. We included public schools in order to ensure a large enough sample. We were not prepared for what we discovered.

We found that at least as many parents of kids in public schools suspected abuse as did parents of kids in private schools. If the parents of a child in a private school blow the whistle on an alleged molester, they can simply put their child in a different school. Furthermore, the school is likely to be responsive because an accusation of abuse can be fatal to a private school. Many parents of kids in public schools were reluctant to raise suspicions about a teacher because their child would probably remain in the school, possibly under the control of the alleged molester. These parents feared that the public school would close ranks behind the accused teacher rather than behind the potentially harmed child.

We had found an important interest group: parents of kids in public schools who suspect abuse but are afraid to speak up. In truth, we had a doubly horrific problem affecting both private and public schools. But realizing that the problem affected a larger set of interests than we initially considered enabled the private school association to take a much stronger stand against abuse in any school. The association used our findings to pass a statewide requirement for strict background checks for *anyone* interacting with children in *any* kind of school. And they were able to educate parents on how to detect the signs of abuse, report concerns, and take prompt, effective action. The actions that the state association took are today's national standard for protecting children from abuse in school.

In this situation, finding hidden interests—the interests of parents of children in public schools—enabled the association to take a leadership position. It was able to make an ethical difference on an issue of critical importance. In other states, private school owners chose to hide from the mostly true allegations, while launching expensive public relations campaigns to burnish their images. By not understanding the interests involved, these private school associations accomplished nothing for themselves or for children in need of protection.

You may think that this situation is unusual, but it isn't. There are hidden interests in most ethical controversies. Some interests are hidden because declaring the interest openly can cause it to be thwarted. This possibility caused the parents of children in public schools to avoid stating their interests. Other interests are hidden because those having the interest do not recognize its relevance or do not have the resources to advocate their interest. In either case, failing to recognize interests may color the facts (it seemed that abuse was happening only in private schools) or make it more difficult to resolve a situation (public schools and private schools working against each other). The right thing to do, attacking abuse in *all* schools, became obvious once the interests in the situation ceased to mask critical facts (abuse was also happening in public schools). Once the interests were on the table, it was easy to see what needed to be done.

TOOL #2 *Reason Backward to Find the Interests*

When considering an ethical issue, how do you know what interests are involved? One thing that often does *not* help is asking those involved what their interests are. Because stating your interests is often associated with *not* achieving them, people are often cautious about revealing their interests. They will state a public or socially acceptable interest but not a more personal or less acceptable interest. Organizations are often even craftier about their interests, putting advocacy of their interests in the hands of public affairs specialists and lobbyists. And it is often the unstated or hidden interests that are the key to resolving ethical issues.

The way to *find the interests* is to reason backwards from an outcome desired by someone to the interest or interests served by that outcome. In other words, ask of each possible outcome, "What interests will that outcome serve and for whom?"

Do not be quick to settle on a single or obvious interest. Most outcomes serve many interests, and there is a tendency to hide a personal interest behind a public interest. For example, in the case of the private and public schools, the public schools were quick to criticize the private schools, apparently in the interest of protecting potentially abused children. And that probably was *one* of their interests. But they were also pursuing a less obvious interest in avoiding scrutiny of their own practices.

Reasoning backwards from outcomes to interests often gives you a good picture of the interests in a situation. But there are also cases in which you will find that there is still something missing. A telltale sign that you are missing some of the interests is that some party to the situation is pushing hard for an outcome that serves no apparent interest.

There are two reasons for not finding relevant interests. There may be hidden *parties* to the situation, like the parents of children in public schools in the case above. Or there may be *outcomes* that have not yet been considered. *Always supplement reasoning backwards by asking, "Who else might be affected?" and "Are there outcomes that haven't been considered?"*

When considering an ethical issue, it is a good idea to list the outcomes under consideration, both declared and undeclared. Once you have listed the outcomes, correlate each one with the interests served by that outcome. Describe the outcomes and related interests as specifically as possible. This will enable you to see if you have understood the interests and outcomes and the connections among them.

Finding the interests allows your ethics sense to help you see what is right. When you know only some of the interests, your ethics sense tries to find a solution based only on those interests. When you have a full picture of the interests, you can view the facts of the situation with less risk of bias and in full knowledge of who may be affected and how.

You can combine *finding the interests with reading the ground rules*. When associating interests with outcomes, you can also associate ground rules with each outcome. Each outcome may not only advance or fail to advance certain interests, it may also be either consistent or inconsistent with the ground rules of the parties to the situation.

We are looking for outcomes that advance many interests without violating the ground rules. Everyone wins and not at the expense of anyone's ethics. We might call such outcomes "win right" outcomes. The parties to the situation "win" in the sense that their interests are advanced. The outcome is "right" in that it does not sacrifice ground rules to advance certain interests.

Is there any guarantee that we will always find a win right solution? Is there any guarantee that there won't be more than one? The answer to both questions is "No." This is where our ethics sense comes into play. *Reading the ground rules* and *finding the interests* are tools to *help* the ethics sense see the right path, even when there isn't a single optimal outcome.

Reading the ground rules and *finding the interests* made it possible to achieve an ethical outcome in the following situation.

SITUATION #5 *Borderline Ethics*

I am often called into situations in which an organization has been caught doing something illegal, unethical, or both. A strategy that organizations employ in these circumstances is to institute a set of practices called an "ethics program" designed to assure the government and the public that the organization can be trusted going forward, no matter what it may have done to date. As an ethics consultant, the situation is ideal in some respects. An organization in serious need of redemption is more likely to listen to an ethics consultant than an organization that is pretty sure that everything it does is right.

I was hired by one such organization, a public hospital located close to the U.S.–Mexico border, seeking an ethics program. Hospitals that serve large numbers of under-insured or uninsured patients sometimes employ a strategy of having medical "residents" deliver many services under the direct supervision of experienced physicians, as opposed to having experienced physicians do all or most of the work themselves. Medical residents have completed their medical education and are serving as residents as part of the process of becoming fully licensed physicians. There is no problem with having services delivered by residents, provided that they are properly supervised. However, the required supervision is expensive so there is a temptation to scrimp on supervision. This hospital had been caught doing just that and was, thus, guilty of improperly taking funds from Medicare and Medicaid. Medicare and Medicaid will pay for services delivered by a resident only if there is documented supervision. I helped the hospital establish an ethics program intended to preclude the delivery of undersupervised services going forward. But this program could do nothing to undo the past.

I joined the hospital's leadership and its attorneys at the offices of the U.S. Department of Justice, where the amount of restitution to be paid to the U.S. government (Medicare and Medicaid) and to others (various states and private insurers) was to be determined. My job was to present the hospital's new ethics program and explain why I believed it would prevent future abuses. We never got that far. The hospital's lawyers were arguing for a comparatively small fine based on technical legal issues. The attorneys for the government not only were not buying, they were becoming furious.

It became clear that the hospital was going up in flames while the lawyers played the fiddle. Despite being guilty in the particulars at issue, this was a good hospital that had helped thousands of individuals who otherwise would have received no care.

During a break, I asked myself what interests the various parties brought to the negotiation. For the government attorneys, the more money they derived from settling the case, the better their performance would be viewed. The hospital's lawyers got paid no matter what happened, but seemed genuinely committed to the hospital's cause. And, I thought about the numerous underserved patients of the hospital, who seemed likely to be even more underserved in the near future.

After the break, I interrupted the ongoing arguments among the attorneys, pleading that I was running out of time. In truth, no one walks out on the Department of Justice. I had decided that it was time to get past the technicalities and focus on the interests. I asked the hospital's new CEO to outline the hospital's financials for the group. The CEO, just as if prepped, apologized for the past improper practices and then outlined the hospital's bleak financial situation showing that 45% of the care it provided was completely uncompensated. One of the lead attorneys for the Department of Justice was of Mexican heritage, and it was as if a light went on for her. If this hospital went down, a lot of people with backgrounds at least somewhat similar to her own would pay for it. She pretty much dismissed the arguments of the hospital's attorneys and proposed a settlement far more reasonable than the hospital considered possible—one that allowed it to continue its charitable mission.

The essence of this case is that it was not just the issues under discussion that were involved. It was the individuals negotiating the issues and the specific interests and ground rules of these individuals. I saw a potential alignment of interests that had nothing to do with the legal merits of the case. The case was not going to trial in any case, so this was a negotiation. I thought that it was worth testing to see if that alignment of interests could overcome the deadlock the parties had argued themselves into.

This case also shows how *finding the interests* in a situation goes hand in hand with *reading the ground rules*. As long as the parties to the negotiation proceeded according to the ground rules of legal process, there was little hope for the hospital. From a legal viewpoint, the hospital was guilty, and any attempt at exculpation was offensive to the government's attorneys. So it was essential to not only broaden interests being considered, but to bring other ground rules, such as those associated with caring for those in need, into the picture. Bringing different interests into play broadened the ground rules relevant to the situation and allowed a solution to be reached.

FACTS MATTER

You may wonder why we haven't talked about assessing the facts in ethical situations. In order for your ethics sense to function properly, you need to have a good grasp of the facts. Unfortunately, the facts don't always speak for themselves.

As we noted earlier, ground rules and, especially, interests influence what the parties to a situation see as facts. In order to assess the actual facts, you have to account for the influence of interests and ground rules. Now that we have looked at ground rules and interests, we can bring fact-finding into the picture. Our next tool helps you sort through the potential bias introduced by the ground rules and interests of the affected parties to get a clear view of the facts.

TOOL #3 *Face the Facts*

The first step in *facing the facts* is to look for the facts that all parties, irrespective of their ground rules and interests, agree upon. This is your core set of facts. In the example above, one such fact was that the hospital had allowed undersupervised services to be delivered by residents. The next step is to identify the contested facts. These are the facts that one party asserts as fundamental, without the agreement of other parties to the situation. In the above example, it was a contested fact whether or not anyone was actually harmed by the undersupervised services. Finally, look at any facts that are introduced by one party but are neither agreed upon nor contested. Thus, facts concerning the financial situation of the hospital were introduced by one party to the situation, the hospital, and not contested by the other parties. Now that you have the universe of facts, it's important to narrow them down to a manageable body of information.

The simplest way to do this is to ask of each contested fact, "If I accepted this as true, would I change my mind about the right thing to do in this situation?" If the answer is no, don't worry about that one. If the answer is yes, evaluating that contested fact may be important to what your ethics sense tells you. If this process does not bring you to a clear picture of the facts relevant to the situation, follow the same process with the facts in the third category, those that are neither agreed upon nor contested.

You have done a good job of *facing the facts* when adding more potential facts to the picture no longer changes what your ethics sense tells you about the correct course of action. There is always a chance that there is some unconsidered fact that will change everything, but you have at least considered all the facts known to the parties to the situation.

Facing the facts is not really a distinct part of the process of finding the right action, as much as it is interwoven with all parts of the process. As you look at the ground rules and interests in a situation, you will find that you constantly have to reevaluate the facts. The same is true with the tools yet to be introduced. As you are using these tools, you will have to reevaluate the facts. As you consider additional facts, the acid test is always the same: If this were true, would it change my judgment as to what is right in the situation? Any fact that fails this test can be safely put aside, at least until some later consideration brings that fact back into the picture.

Chapter Three

The Ethics Eye

"Vision: Something seen otherwise than by ordinary sight . . ."
—Webster's Collegiate Dictionary, 5th Edition

We now have three tools for resolving ethical issues. They are reading the ground rules, finding the interests, and facing the facts. These tools help us find the substance of an ethical issue, as opposed to what is said about the issue, and may even resolve the issue in some cases.

We have also looked at a number of actual situations. The common theme is that although these situations involved ethical issues, once we applied our tools, we could see the right course of action. It is reasonable to ask whether this is simply because of the situations selected or whether there is another reason. I believe that these cases become clear primarily because we have an innate ethics sense that allows us to see what is right. *Reading the ground rules, finding the interests,* and *facing the facts* make it easier for this innate ethics sense to function. I call this innate ethics sense the "ethics eye." Far from being a mysterious power, the ethics eye is a natural extension of certain basic human traits. Its role in ethical reasoning was noted as early as the eighteenth century by Adam Smith, best known as the author of *The Wealth of Nations*.[2] We introduce a tool in this chapter that makes it even easier for the ethics eye to function accurately.

CONTROVERSY AND THE ETHICS SENSE

Given the depth of division over many ethical issues, it may seem unlikely that there is an innate ability to tell right from wrong. If there is an innate ability to see what is right, why do arguments over right and wrong so often end with the very same disagreement with which they began? Who ever resolved a dispute over a serious ethical matter, except through the use of force?

This kind of thinking often leads us to throw up our hands when facing a challenging ethical issue, whether it is abortion, euthanasia, the treatment of terrorist prisoners, assigning the responsibility for an oil spill, bribing foreign officials as a condition of doing business, or any of the ethical issues that arise in our daily work lives. It is considered a sign of worldliness to say that some cultures and viewpoints are "just different." It has gotten to the point where many of us are ashamed to take a firm ethical stand. To say that something is just plain right or wrong seems narrow-minded.

On the other hand, there are those who avoid discussing ethical issues because there is no point in doing so outside of a "correct" religious or political viewpoint. Rather than engage in practical discourse on ethical issues, they fall back on an unquestioned authority. When we put the relativistic and authoritarian approaches to ethics together, we have rendered ourselves mute on some of the most significant issues of our time.

Remember that deep, recalcitrant arguments and divisions are not unique to ethics. They are common to such fields as physics (particles, waves, strings), cosmology (big bang, steady state), and psychology (cognitivism, behaviorism). The fact that we have these recalcitrant disagreements does not lead us to distrust our senses. In fact, it often leads us to seek innovative tools to strengthen the senses. The telescope does not replace the eye; it makes it able to see more.

At least some controversies in science are *eventually* resolved. In ethics nothing ever seems to be resolved.

One of the reasons that scientific controversies are sometimes resolved is simply that we are willing to count them as resolved. There are still people who believe in astrology, a version of Ptolemaic astronomy. This does not lead us to conclude the scientific dispute between Copernicus and Ptolemy was never resolved. Similarly, there are people who believe there are circumstances in which infanticide is ethical. Shouldn't we trust ourselves to say as more than a matter of opinion that infanticide is wrong?

One of the reasons we are perplexed by ethical disagreements is not because they are insoluble but because we don't know what would count as resolving them. When we learn something in physics, we understand that what we have learned is subject to revision or even rejection at a later time. Even in mathematics, one day's basic truth is the next day's old school superstition. For example, all of mathematics as we know it is based on the idea that logic has two values, true and false. And yet physics teaches us that this cannot be the case if we are to allow for quantum phenomena. In other words, even in science and mathematics, today's unshakeable truth is tomorrow's ignorant myth.

We seem unwilling to grant our ethical viewpoints this same right to revision based on new learning. In other words, we seem to require that ethical truth be universally acknowledged, not subject to revision, and eternally true. This is because we don't know what it would mean to learn more or gather additional evidence in ethics. But once we understand how our ethics sense operates, we will see that it is possible to learn more in ethics and to revise ethical viewpoints as progress is made.

What Is the Ethics Sense?

If controversy and disagreement do not rule out an ethics sense, what is the ethics sense? How does it relate to the five physical senses? Is it a special sense like the aesthetic sense that we are told is a gift to a select few? Is it like the sense of balance, which goes completely unnoticed as long as it works?

Two famous psychology experiments shed light on the ethics sense. These experiments were not conducted to establish the ethics sense. But their results give insight into the ethics sense.

The first is called the Milgram experiment.[3] While this experiment is usually cited to show how authority may excessively influence decision making, it also demonstrates how the ethics sense works.

Here is what happened in the Milgram experiment.

Stanley Milgram, a Yale University psychologist, conducted an experiment in which a volunteer (the "teacher") was instructed as part of the experiment to deliver an electric shock to a subject (the "learner") when the subject gave the wrong answer to a multiple-choice question. The volunteers believed that "teachers" and "learners" were randomly assigned their roles, but the "learners" were actually Milgram's associates. The "learner" was placed in another room where the "learner" could not be observed or heard by the "teacher." The "teacher" was instructed to shock the "learner" each time the "learner" gave an incorrect response. The level of the shock increased with each incorrect response, ranging from a modest 15 volts up to a monstrous 450 volts. The 450-volt shock was described to the "teacher" as a "dangerous severe shock." The "teacher" was even given a mild shock so he would get a sense of what the "learner" experienced when the "teacher" delivered a shock. Unbeknownst to the "teachers," no real shocks were delivered to the "learners," who could not be observed by the "teachers."

For each trial, the "teacher" was supervised by a confederate of Milgram dressed in a lab coat to convey the sense that he was an authority. "Teachers" were reminded of the importance of the experiment and told that not completing the trial in which they were participating would invalidate the whole study. Most of the "teachers" eventually administered huge "shocks" to the "learners." At 300 volts, some of the "learners" were told to kick and scream loudly enough to be heard through the wall by the "teachers." A few "teachers" objected or dropped out of the experiment at this point, but most of the "teachers" ended up delivering the maximum shock of 450 volts to the "learners." The experiment, which has been replicated several times, has been taken to show the extent to which an authority figure—the person in the lab coat—can persuade otherwise normal individuals to inflict terrible pain on others. And there is no argument with this conclusion.

Philip Zimbardo, a Stanford psychologist, conducted a related experiment.[4]

Zimbardo divided a group of volunteers into two groups of equal size, the "guards" and the "prisoners." The volunteers were told that they would participate in a two-week simulation of prison life. Both "guards" and "prisoners" received uniforms appropriate to their roles. The uniforms given to "prisoners" were even more demeaning than those used in real prisons. "Guards" received "training" on the essentials of their roles, while prisoners were given prisoner numbers and cell assignments. "Guards" were told to maintain obedience on the part of "prisoners," while "prisoners" were addressed only by their numbers. A prison "warden" and "superintendent" (Zimbardo himself) were also appointed. All of this occurred in a mock prison in the basement of a Stanford University building. All participants could leave the premises at any time, without needing anyone's permission, and yet none did so. (Some volunteers experienced such high levels of distress that they were "released" early by Zimbardo.) The volunteers were so committed to their roles that "guards" struck "prisoners" with billy sticks and forced them to clean toilets with their bare hands—and the "prisoners" complied. The experiment was terminated after six days when a respected individual not connected with the experiment observed how far things had gone and told Zimbardo to stop the experiment before someone was seriously harmed.

At the time of these experiments there was active public discussion of the excuse offered by several prominent Nazi war criminals (Adolf Eichman, Albert Spier) that they had acted in obedience to irresistible pressure from higher authorities. Their argument was that those who sat in judgment of them would have done the same things were they under the same pressures. And there is no question that these experiments show a frightening human tendency to capitulate to authority, sometimes enthusiastically. But that is not our point in reviewing these experiments.

In follow-up studies to Milgram's experiment, Milgram found that the willingness of "teachers" to shock "learners" decreased in direct proportion to the extent to which the "teacher" was in the physical presence of the "learner." The "teacher" became progressively less willing to shock the "learner" as the "teacher" could see, hear, or touch the "learner." Milgram observed, "It is possible that the visual cues associated with the victim's suffering trigger empathetic responses in the subject and give him a more complete grasp of the victim's experience. . . . Diminishing obedience, then, would be explained by the enrichment of empathetic cues in the successive experimental conditions."[5]

The Zimbardo experiment teaches a related lesson. Once again we saw individuals surrendering their judgment to a role-based authority. It is interesting that Zimbardo himself, contrary to every rule of experimental procedure, became similarly attached to his role as "prison superintendent." Fearing a "breakout" at one point during the experiment, he wanted to transfer the subjects cast as "prisoners" to a city jail and became irate when the city would not go along with this harebrained scheme. The experiment only ended because someone not connected with it—and highly regarded by Zimbardo—took an objective look at what was happening. An outsider could easily see that the situation had evolved into one capable of causing serious harm to the participants. This outsider called on Zimbardo's professional respect and personal regard to jar Zimbardo to his senses.

These experiments give insight into our ethics sense. It is this ethics sense that Milgram is reaching for when he talks about "empathetic cues." Receiving empathetic cues could not have *caused* the "teachers" to relent. Most "teachers" did not relent, and a sociopathic individual would not have responded at all to these cues. The question is, what were these cues *to* if they were not cues to the ethics sense of the "teachers"? Why should we be less willing to inflict pain on another just because we have a better sense of what we are doing? The reason is that the cues trigger the ethics sense of normal individuals. When the subjects received empathic cues, their ethics sense showed some of them that it was wrong to administer further shocks. In other words, the subjects did not stop delivering shocks just because of the empathetic cues. They stopped because these cues showed some of them that delivering more shocks was wrong.

It is important to distinguish between the empathetic cues and the "teachers'" reaction to these cues. "Empathy" is defined as "the power of entering into the experience of or understanding objects of emotions outside of ourselves."[6] It is perfectly clear that "teachers" who entered into the experience of "learners," while less likely to shock them, were still able and, in some cases, quite willing to do so. While the ethics eye of these individuals was brought somewhat into focus by the empathetic cues, it was still *separate from* these cues. If the ethics sense were *not separate* from the cues, none of the subjects would have continued to administer high levels of shock.

In the Zimbardo experiment, the barriers between the "guards" and the "prisoners" and between the "superintendent" and everyone else were entirely psychological, although equally powerful as the physical barriers in Milgram's experiment. In other words, it is reasonable to believe that Zimbardo, for example, even though in the role of "prison superintendent," was able to be empathetic with respect to the participants in his experiment. It was not that he needed to be more in the role of the other participants; he needed to *care more* about what happened to the participants in these roles. The outsider who stopped Zimbardo from continuing the experiment released him not from the limits of his empathetic imagination, but from the limitations of his *sympathetic* feelings for the participants.

If being empathetic with another is being able to put yourself in the other's position, being sympathetic with another is being able to feel what others feel in a given situation. I am using "sympathy" not in the narrow sense in which the suffering of another causes you to suffer. I am using it in the sense of the definition as "a (real or supposed) affinity between certain things, by virtue of which they are similarly or correspondingly affected by the same influence."[7] In other words, I may be in sympathy with the *good feelings* of others as well as their miseries. When Zimbardo's associate jogged him loose from his role in the experiment, his ability to *feel* what the participants in the experiment were feeling kicked in. And once he felt as they did, his ethics sense told him to stop.

DISTANCE DISARMS ETHICS

Being sympathetic and empathetic toward others are key factors that focus the ethics sense. It is often noted that many of us could push a button to drop a bomb on a city, although few of us could go through the city killing the self-same people by stabbing them. What makes it hard to kill with your hands, as opposed to dropping a bomb, is that the presence of the person engages your sympathy, empathy, and ethics sense.

A good way to summarize what the experiments teach us is that when distance from others weakens our abilities to empathize or sympathize with them, the functioning of our ethics eye is impaired. While this distance may be physical (a wall, a barrier, or just sheer distance), it may also be the distance created by roles or categories that sort people into kinds (teacher, learner, guard, prisoner). The tools that sharpen the ethics eye, such as seeing situations in terms of interests and ground rules, are ways to better put ourselves in the situations of others in both empathetic and sympathetic terms. If you know the ground rules of others, you will be better able see a situation as they see it in terms of right and wrong. If you are aware of the interests involved in a situation, you have a better idea of the feelings that others bring to the situation.

Think about how we came to have an ethics sense. The basic wiring of human beings has not changed since we emerged from caves and learned to make fire. Just as early humans had the five recognized senses, so they also experienced emotions such as fear, love, and sorrow. While man has progressed since those early days, there is no reason to think that the basic senses and emotional makeup of humans have changed. When humans emerged from caves, there was a great need for cooperation within a hunter-gatherer group. To tighten the bonds of cooperation within such a group, it was advantageous for group members to imagine and feel the pain and suffering of one another. The ability to sympathize and empathize created commitment and solidarity within the group. This is likely how ethics emerged. To ensure cooperation within a group, certain ground rules about how group members were to be treated created reliable expectations among group members.

On the other hand, it was also advantageous to be able to put aside these feelings when dealing with outsiders who might threaten the a group. If one was forced to defend the group against its enemies, the ability to put aside sympathy and empathy regarding an enemy became adaptive. Because characteristics that could identify an outsider as a threat to a group were not necessarily physical (they are bigger) or sensory (they smell different), we developed the ability to *decide* to whom we would extend what has been called "fellow feeling." Armies would not wear distinctive uniforms if the uniforms did not help soldiers "decide" who the enemy was. If we decide that others who differ from us by age, race, gender, nationality, or role are distant from us, our empathetic and sympathetic feelings toward them are weakened. In some individuals the remaining feelings of sympathy or empathy are sufficient to give them qualms about injuring "outsiders." But the ethics sense of many allows harm or injury to those judged as "outsiders."

This way of looking at things helps us better understand the case of the border hospital (Situation #5). When I looked at the situation from the viewpoint of the government attorney, I realized that she had decided that this was a justice (in this case, personified by the U.S. Department of Justice) versus the wrong-doer (the hospital) situation, and she was reacting from her professional role as "defender of justice." When I thought about the interests involved in the case, I saw that a commonality of interests between the attorney and the hospital might lead her to a view that allowed her ethics sense to function more fully with respect to the hospital.

TOOL #4   *Stand in the Shoes*

In the early 1980s, Tom Peters and Bob Waterman wrote a book, *In Search of Excellence,* which changed American business—for the better.[8] The book is about the common characteristics of companies that are successful over a long period of time. The main lesson that I and many other readers took away from the book became known as "Management by Walking Around." The idea behind this concept, which became a series of speeches, calendars, baubles, and, of course, follow-up books, was that domestic companies were failing because their leaders had lost touch with their own employees and customers. For example, if the leaders of domestic car companies had spent time in their companies' repair docks, showrooms, and break rooms, they would not have needed Japanese competitors to refocus their attention on quality and service. Using surveys and other tools instead of actually talking to customers and employees is just another way of keeping them at arm's length. In short, the message was to walk around and talk to your employees and customers to learn what they really want as opposed to what Marketing and Human Resources tell you they want. Many CEOs allocated a fixed part of their weekly schedule to walking around and talking to employees and customers. Michael Bloomberg, mayor of New York City, is one of the best known proponents of this approach. That is why he sits in a "bull pen" shoulder to shoulder with his direct reports and sometimes rides public transportation to work.

Given what we have learned about the way distance reduces empathy and sympathy, we can see why Management by Walking Around works. When you get to know people as individuals, as opposed to roles or categories, the distance between you and them decreases and your ability to see and feel their circumstances increases. They cease being the *role* of employee or the *role* of customer and become people. You get to know what they want and how to make things, including products and services, that work for them. As you increase your ability to share their thoughts and feelings, the ethics eye has an opportunity to function.

There are many examples of how this works. I grew up in a small town in which there was one black family. They were fairly well-off as they ran a funeral home that catered to black people in a nearby, larger city. Until I was fifteen or sixteen, I had never known a black person. I grew up in the Italian ghetto of the same city and borders were not crossed. I was an avid golfer, and one day, Davy, a teenage boy from this one black family, and I ended up playing together. I found out that he and I had more in common than most of the kids with whom I normally played. I learned a lot about race and racism and about the way it uses distance to stunt our ethics sense. It is a *decision*, a reprehensible one, to make people of a different race (ethnicity, gender, age, religion, sexual orientation) "outsiders" and not within the full scope of our ethics sense.

There is nothing remarkable about this story. Everyone has stories in which circumstances forced them to get to know someone who differed from them in a key characteristic, a characteristic designed to make them "other" to the ethics sense. Generally, we draw the lesson that there is no good reason for maintaining distance from these formerly "unlike" people, and we begin to share their experiences and feelings. But we may miss the bigger lesson of how distance, including the distance we create, reduces our ability to see the right thing and do it.

If you want your innate ethics sense, your ethics eye, to lead you to sound ethical decisions, you have to learn to *stand in the shoes* of those affected by your actions. When you get to know people as individuals, the distance between you and them decreases and your ability to see and feel the situation increases. They cease being the *role* of employee or the *role* of customer and become people. You get to know what they want and how that fits or doesn't fit what you want. As you increase your ability to share their thoughts and feelings, you gain the ability to see ethical situations as others do. You also lose the ability to treat them with indifference, as "outsiders" with respect to your ethics sense.

It takes discipline to sharpen your ethics eye to the point where you can stand in the shoes of others. When you approach a situation that poses an ethical issue, identify the individuals and groups potentially affected by what happens. This is a natural extension of *finding the interests,* since you are now giving an identity to those who have the interests.

Now that you know who is affected, reduce the distance between you and them. *Identify the affected individuals and groups that differ from you the most and meet the individuals or members of the group.* It may surprise you that seeing the right course of action requires that you leave the couch, but it does. "Walk around" your ethical situation until you have had meaningful, face-to-face contact with the main parties to the issue. In some cases, it will be practically impossible to meet these individuals or groups. If you cannot meet with some of the parties personally, read something written by or about individuals of that kind. Think of not allowing yourself to become the "teacher" shocking the "learner" or to fall into a role ("prison guard"). Just as business leaders tend to be lazy about getting to know workers and customers, we tend to be lazy about getting to know those who may be affected by our actions. But *this is what you have to do to see the right course of action.*

List the affected individuals and groups most distant from you and write down their interests and ground rules, particularly ground rules that differ from your own. You will know that you have completed the task of reducing your distance from them if you are able to verify or reject each interest and ground rule. Of course, you will add interests and modify ground rules throughout the process. *You are removing obstacles to the functioning of your ethics eye by bringing its objects closer.* If you follow this process conscientiously, you gain confidence in your ethical decisions and in your ability to make an ethical difference. You have created conditions in which your ethics eye works.

Let's see how this works in a complex situation.

SITUATION #6 *Kneecapped*

I worked as a professor before devoting full time to being an ethics advisor. Even then, I was known for my interest in ethics. One day I got a call from a Dr. Cullen (name changed) wanting to meet with me about an ethical issue. Even if you are interested in ethics, you are not necessarily interested in everyone's ethical problems. But Dr. Cullen was persistent, and when I learned that he was an M.D. and the new head of the university's student health service, my interest was piqued. I expected a problem about student health coverage for birth control or parental notification of abortions or one of the other issues typical of student health. I did not get what I expected.

Over the weekend, a member of the school's football team had visited the student health center, for some reason not going to the team doctor. He had a sore knee. Dr. Cullen was the only physician on duty and examined the young man's knee. What he found was startling. Someone had performed *non-arthroscopic* surgery on the student's knee. The surgery was archaic and sloppy and would have to be redone with a medium prospect of success. This young athlete was the first member of his family to attend college, and he was expected to turn pro when he completed school. He would earn enough to change the circumstances of his family forever. Except for the knee.

When Dr. Cullen reported this to the team doctor, the team doctor told Dr. Cullen that he was an inexperienced general practitioner and was mistaken. When Dr. Cullen reported the situation to the athletic director, he was told to take a hike.

We again have a situation in which the facts don't add up. On the face of it, Dr. Cullen was simply trying to help a student athlete. Dr. Cullen was young, bright, and self-assured, and so I thought that maybe a know-it-all manner explained his cold reception. I did some research.

I learned that the athletic director had a football team booster group composed of local doctors, who paid $20,000 a year each to be part of this group. There was no qualification for joining this group except that one be a physician willing to fork over $20,000. In return for their $20,000, the booster physicians got good seats, a chance to meet the players, and one more thing—they got most of the medical referrals when the athletic department's own staff couldn't handle a problem. The incompetent doctor who operated on the young athlete's knee belonged to this group. I could see why no one wanted to talk to Dr. Cullen.

I told Dr. Cullen that I saw two options. The first was to bring the press into the picture. This would certainly ruin his career at the university, and probably elsewhere. Since I had become a "known associate" of Dr. Cullen, my career would be on shaky ground, too. On the other hand, the story could easily be confirmed, and it would be front-page news in the local press, and probably nationally. This is what I call the "power option," which means forcing people to do the right thing whether or not they want to. There are times when the power option is the only or best option.

Another option was to go straight to the president of the university. The president, who was relatively new to his position, could take the high ground by addressing the problem forthrightly. The problem was that the athletic director had been the new president's first significant appointment, so the president was at considerable risk himself.

Dr. Cullen told me that he had already written to the president and showed me the letter, which was argumentative and disrespectful. Dr. Cullen was angry and it showed. I feared that the president had reacted more to the tone of his letter than to its contents. As a newly appointed professor, I was hardly a power player. If we were going to have a chance, we needed a good strategy.

I decided on another letter to the president, this time with a polite and respectful tone. I was pretty sure he would not read another letter from Dr. Cullen so the task fell to me. I stated in my letter that as a new faculty member, I wanted nothing more than to see my school do the right thing.

The strategy worked well enough for me to get a half-hour appointment with the president. But instead of showing up alone, I brought along Dr. Cullen, the student athlete, and the athlete's parents. The president was furious with me but met with everyone, as he had little choice. You could almost see the light go on while he was trying to explain things to the parents. Sympathy and empathy kicked in and jarred him out of his institutional role. The student athlete ceased being a thorny problem and became a wronged person. The last piece was to assure the president that the story would go no further. In the space of that half hour, he got the process of doing the right thing in motion.

When we realize that others have the ethics eye, a new strategy becomes available to us. Not only can we sharpen our own ethical insight, we can *create circumstances that bring the ethics eyes of others into focus.* In the above situation, this was accomplished by bringing several of the affected parties into the presence of the decision maker. It was enough to clear his vision. This strategy of sharpening the ethics eye of others is the key to building ethical agreement and taking effective action.

Chapter Four

Not in My Backyard

"If the ends don't justify the means, what does?"

—unattributed

"The greatest happiness of the greatest number is the foundation of morals and legislation."

—Jeremy Bentham (*Works*, Vol. X, p. 142)

SITUATION #7 *Judge for Yourself*

In a seminar for a group of state judges, one of the judges asked the following question: "What would you do if you were the judge and the prosecution brought someone before the court who was clearly guilty of the charges against him—and any number of other serious crimes, mostly against the elderly?" The problem is that the prosecution made a "technical error" by not showing the defense certain key documents. This probably happened because the case was so open-and-shut against the defendant that someone got sloppy. In a practical sense, there is no question about the guilt of the defendant. The defense does not know about the missing documents and need never know about them. The judge should throw the case out on a procedural error. The problem is that this will put the culprit back on the street for an indefinite period of time, unquestionably hurting people.

Should the judge overlook the error by the prosecution in the interest of public safety? Use this chapter's tool to find a solution and compare your solution with the one at the end of the chapter.

If you asked an economist how to tell right from wrong, she would probably tell you to determine which action will yield the best consequences. On this view, rightness depends not on our sense of right and wrong, but on a sort of global cost-benefit analysis. You can be sure that an action is right if it will produce the greatest balance of benefit over harm for all concerned. Why do something that "seems right" according to your ethics sense if you can create more benefit by doing something else? On this view, instead of trying to "see" what is right, we need economists, policy makers, and scientists to help us predict the course of action that will lead to the greatest benefit.

THE GLOBAL BENEFIT APPROACH

This idea of maximizing benefit seems simple and logical, and it is in the DNA of today's policy makers. There are consulting firms that do nothing other than cost-benefit analyses designed to show how a particular policy will, or will not, produce the greatest benefit. Let's call this approach the *global benefit approach,* because the overall benefit of doing something is its ethics gold standard.

No question, there is something to learn from the *global benefit approach*. But far from replacing our ethics sense, the *global benefit approach* is a natural ally of the ethics eye. In fact, the *global benefit approach* will give us one of our most powerful tools for sharpening the ethics eye.

Like a lot of ideas that seem simple at first, the *global benefit approach* is not so simple. It has serious limitations.

One limitation has to do with the fact that some actions not only produce benefit, they also produce harm. For example, a developer who wants to build a casino in what has been a quiet suburban neighborhood can point to many likely benefits. The casino will produce a flood of needed revenue while creating hundreds of jobs and providing an entertainment outlet for the area.

Our first thought is that there must be other, better locations for the casino. Why ruin a perfectly good neighborhood to gain the benefits of a casino? The developer's answer is that this is the best location *in the area*. If the people in this area want the benefits of the casino, they will have to accept the costs.

The residents of the neighborhood are appalled at the idea of a casino in their backyard. It will ruin the very features that make the neighborhood a desirable place to live, attract all sorts of outsiders, produce a mountain of litter, and create traffic havoc.

This is a common debate across society where people favor some benefit-producing activity (a factory, a shopping mall, a homeless shelter) just as long as it is "not in my backyard." If we were to settle the casino issue on the *global benefit approach*, the neighborhood would lose. The harm affecting a *small number* of residents cannot compare to the benefits of the casino to a much *larger number* of people in the area. If this conclusion makes you a bit queasy, you are beginning to see the limits to the *global benefit approach.*

If you are like me, you think the neighbors have rights. Your ethics eye tells you that you just don't mow people down in the name of increased revenues. And you may even question the benefits. Just because you can measure the revenue to be produced by the casino doesn't mean it is more valuable than preserving a neighborhood. And one of the reasons we have rules is so that the interests of the many don't trample the rights of the few.

This shows that the *global benefit approach* only works if you establish certain things up front, things that the ethics eye can help establish.

A project I participated in as part of consulting team illustrates what you need to clarify up front. Our client was a state legislature. The state legislature wanted the consultants to do a cost-benefit analysis of whether the shore of the state should be developed for industrial or recreational purposes. The consultants immediately ran into problems. How do you weigh the benefits of a day at the beach against the benefits of a day's pay? Do only current state residents count or should we consider those who will move in from other states to take advantage of the jobs/recreation? How many generations into the future should be considered?

WHO COUNTS—WHAT COUNTS

To use the *global benefit approach* you need to answer two questions up front—*who counts* and *what counts.* You need to know *who counts* as part of "everyone," when assessing the benefits for everyone. Many disagreements arise because one policymaker thinks "everyone" means everyone who can vote in their district, while another wants to count a hundred generations into the future. You see this in debates over fossil fuels where advocates are thinking mainly in terms of current generations, while opponents want to consider generations far into the future.

Similar issues arise when you try to figure out *what counts* as a benefit or harm. If you count only things that can be quantified in terms of dollars and cents, you end up building a lot of casinos. You also end up with the sense that a lot has been left out of the picture.

Instead of being an alternative to an innate ethics sense, the *global benefit approach* is best viewed as a tool to sharpen the ethics eye. The *global benefit approach* aids the ethics eye by making us look at the consequences of our actions in terms of two questions. First, we have to ask who counts to be sure that the relevant parties are considered. Second, we have to ask what counts as a benefit or harm. Asking these questions will often bring us closer to seeing the right course of action, particularly in situations involving many options.

TOOL #5 *The Global Benefit Approach*

The *global benefit approach* doesn't solve ethical problems, but it raises questions that can help solve these problems. Even if you cannot tell if something is right just by asking if it produces the greatest benefit, the benefit an action produces is relevant to its rightness. Once we realize this, the *global benefit approach* becomes a powerful tool to sharpen the ethics eye.

The *global benefit approach* is especially effective in business situations where you have to justify your approach. Usually you can't just say what you believe is right without justifying your viewpoint. You can often use the *global benefit approach* to support your viewpoint.

In order to use the *global benefit approach* you first have to ask *who counts—who* are the affected parties. You also have to ask *what* is to be considered—*what counts* as a benefit or harm.

Who counts? If you have already used *find the interests,* you have a good understanding of who counts—the individuals and groups with an interest in a situation. You also have to ask *what* is to be considered as a benefit or harm. If you have used *stand in the shoes,* you have a good idea what counts—that which would count as a benefit or harm if you stood in the shoes of the potentially affected parties.

Our first tool, *reading the ground rules,* also fits into the *global benefit approach.* While we want to produce as much benefit as possible, we also have to consider the ground rules that apply to what we are doing. An action that produces a lot of benefit while violating important ground rules is probably not the right action. An action that produces great benefit without violating the ground rules is, however, a good candidate for being the right action.

Look again at the neighborhood casino. When we ask who is relevant to the decision, the answer is easy—everyone who will be benefited or harmed by the casino. To this point, the casino looks like a clear winner since so many will benefit (everyone who benefits from the increased tax revenue and new jobs) compared to the much smaller number (current residents of the neighborhood) who will be harmed. However, when we look at the ground rules, we quickly see that some basic ground rules will be violated if the casino proceeds. One of these ground rules states that a person's right to his property and his home normally should not be abridged without his consent. If the casino developer were being honest, he would admit that he upholds this same ground rule *with respect to his own home and property.* In fact, stuffing the casino down the throats of the neighborhood is so contrary to the ground rules that enable communities to function that it is not an acceptable outcome. Of course, there might be situations in which the developer would be right (the benefits are greater) and the neighborhood wrong (there is less disruption), but this is not one of them.

One of the limitations of the ethics eye is that our own ability to sympathize and empathize with others is limited. We tend to think of those most like us and closest at hand. Like *stand in the shoes,* the *global benefit approach* helps remedy this nearsightedness. It forces us to look more broadly at the consequences of our actions. If we add the *global benefit approach* to our list of tools, we will know that we have taken account of the consequences.

SITUATION #7 *Judge for Yourself (continued)*

Our judge wants to know if he should violate the rules of court procedure to prevent harm to the community. In short, his question is, "What is more important, the rules of the court or the good of the community?" The judge thinks that the *global benefit approach* directs him to ignore court procedure and allow the prisoner to be found guilty "for the good of the community." Now that we know that the *global benefit approach* cannot give an answer by itself, we can see what is wrong with this line of thinking. If the judge allows the prisoner to be found guilty, he violates a ground rule he is sworn to uphold, which is that judges should uphold the law regardless of their personal opinions. This ground rule itself provides great benefit to the community. When you supplement the *global benefit approach* with *reading the ground rules,* you see that the judge should not free the prisoner. The judge is too focused on the potential short-term harm that may be caused by releasing the prisoner to consider the potentially greater harm of having judges violate court procedure as they see fit. On the other hand, the judge does have an obligation to use his position to call on other resources to protect the community from the prisoner if the prisoner is released.

Chapter Five

Uncommon Sense

"The man who never alters his opinion is like standing water, and breeds reptiles of the mind."

—William Blake, *Plate 7*

Some people have difficulty recognizing the ethics sense, even after using this sense to solve problems. This is usually because the idea of an ethics sense seems to conflict with two of their beliefs. The first is that it should it be easier to resolve ethical disputes if we have an ethics sense. The second is that the idea of an ethics sense seems contrary to common sense or science.

We have observed that difficult controversies are not unique to ethics, nor do they prove that there is no innate ethical ability. Such controversies only show that our innate ethics sense, much like our other senses, requires tools to increase its effectiveness. Still, it would be nice to go beyond this and show how the ethics eye helps resolve difficult controversies. We look at how to move beyond controversy to ethical agreement and action in the next two chapters

In this chapter, I address the idea that the ethics eye is mysterious or unscientific. There are many different ways in which common sense or science might seem to conflict with there being an innate ethics sense. The following questions express some common objections to the ethics sense.

1. If we have this sense, why are we not (more) aware of it?

2. Our senses have a physiological basis in the brain. Doesn't this leave the ethics eye out?

3. If there is an ethics sense, wouldn't two people looking at the same situation "see" the same action as right?

Answering these questions not only removes objections to the ethics eye, it begins the process of showing how to use the ethics eye to build consensus with others.

AWARENESS OF THE ETHICS SENSE

The first question is, "If we have an ethics sense, why are we not (more) aware of it?" This question assumes that we are aware of all of our senses, but this is not true. For example, we are ordinarily not aware of our sense of balance. We can become aware of our sense of balance if it is disturbed, but it is not ordinarily within our awareness. And even though we are not ordinarily aware of our sense of balance, there are exercises we can do to sharpen it. For example, learning to maintain one's balance while standing on an inflated ball definitely brings your sense of balance into awareness and sharpens it in the process. There are other candidates for senses of which we are not immediately aware such as an aesthetic sense, our ability to learn language (our language sense), and our sense of self or identity.

We also saw earlier how the ethics eye does come into our awareness when those affected by our actions are within our sight, hearing, and touch. When the "teachers" in Milgram's experiment came into closer contact with the "learners," they found it harder to shock them. Even those who delivered the maximum shock to subjects in Milgram's experiment reported being deeply disturbed by their actions when debriefed. While there was no longer anything for the "teachers" to empathize with once the "teacher" could no longer shock the "learner," the "teacher's" ethics sense (of wrongness) was still prominent in their experience. When we heighten our sympathy and empathy, our ethics sense surfaces. And once it has come to the surface, it keeps us focused on the rightness or wrongness of our actions even after sympathy and empathy fade.

If the ethics sense is like our other senses, individuals will have it to varying degrees. If true saints are at one end of the ethics spectrum, then sociopaths occupy the end reserved for the ethically blind. Again, since all of our human senses are subject to varying degrees of acuity, it is not surprising that there are disagreements about ethics depending on the differing acuity of the ethics sense of different individuals. If I literally do not see the harm in what I am doing, even if it has been explained to me, I will not think that what I am doing is wrong.

Interlude: Pass the Guilt, Please

One sign of the functioning of the ethics eye is the experience of remorse or guilt. While guilt is a difficult emotion to analyze, there is no question that individuals feel varying degrees of guilt when they act contrary to their ethics sense. We can see that guilt is tied to the ethics eye since guilt often persists long after any feelings of sympathy or empathy have dissolved.

The role of guilt in ethics is much debated. The philosopher Friedrich Nietzsche viewed guilt as a tool by which the weaker elements of society control the stronger. When the weak cannot control the stronger by force, they rely on a sense of guilt or sin on the part of the stronger to keep them under the control of the weaker. Some psychologists associate guilt with rationalization. When a people do wrong, the fact that they are "punished" by their own guilt makes it easier for them to accept what they have done—and, perhaps, to do it again. In most religions, guilt plays the role of restoring a sense of balance or harmony when one has done wrong or sinned. This guilt is relieved by repenting, which in turn clears the way for honest action in the future.

This much is certain. Guilt is mainly oriented toward the past, toward what we have already thought and done. You can't feel guilty about something unless you have done it or at least contemplated doing it. However, when we are considering what we should do, we sometimes ask ourselves, "Would I feel guilty if I went ahead and did that?" We are trying to measure the correctness of an action by how we might feel once it occurs.

When you look at guilt in terms of future actions, you can see that guilt, and its close associate, remorse, play the role of reminders of how you felt about doing certain things in the past. Guilt is a signpost to remind a person—You'll feel guilty if you do this!—not to do wrong when one's own ethics sense is not strong enough to ensure choice of the right path.

Even though guilt is sometimes provoked by the ethics eye, it is an inexact indicator of right and wrong. Some people feel guilt easily and even feel guilt when there is nothing for them to feel guilty about. This is the neurotic guilt of the overactive superego. Others may commit all kinds of thoughtless or wrong actions and have only the slightest sense of guilt or remorse, if any. The role of guilt is to substitute for good ethical judgment—for the operation of the ethics eye. But you are much better off getting your innate ethics sense into focus rather than relying on the erratic emotion of guilt to show you right and wrong. If we work to make our ethics eye operate as accurately as possible, we are better off than if we are relying on a guilty conscience to punish us once we have already done something that is wrong.

BRAIN ETHICS

Our second question asks, "Our senses have a physiological basis in the brain. Does this leave the ethics eye out?"

The mapping of brain functions to thoughts and actions is in its early stages. For example, while there is a general sense of what part of the brain supports vision, it is still unclear how sight and touch work together in complex human actions. It is also increasingly clear that the brain has "emergent" characteristics. In other words, many higher level brain functions depend on patterns affecting many parts of the brain concurrently, as opposed to a single area. For example, the experience of love may involve areas of the brain associated with sight, hearing, memory, pleasure, language, and imagination operating in concert. There probably is not a single love node in the brain.

It is likely that the ethics sense is one of the complex or emergent activities of the brain that involve multiple areas. For example, the ability to be empathetic certainly involves imagination (of another person's situation), which has several sensory components such as visual, auditory, tactile, and emotional elements. To experience things as another person experiences them requires us to imagine what the other person is experiencing. Similarly, the ability to be sympathetic, to feel some of what others are feeling, requires imagining another's situation well enough that your own feelings mimic those of the person actually experiencing the situation. Since the ethics sense comes into play when the abilities to sympathize and empathize are heightened, it is a safe bet that the ethics sense also involves many areas of the brain.

Even at our current primitive stage of brain mapping, there are brain states associated with sympathy and empathy. And the most recent research does indeed loosely associate the areas of the brain in which these states occur with ethical judgment.[9] In fact, there is current research on conflict resolution and cooperation, both related to our ethics sense, focusing on these and other areas of the brain.

We hardly know enough to conclude that the brain has no room for the ethics sense. What we do know about the brain makes it highly likely that the ethics sense involves multiple areas of the brain. Since we do make ethical judgments, a fuller understanding of the brain is bound to accommodate the ethics eye.

SHARPER VISION

Our final question asks, "If there is an ethics sense, wouldn't two people looking at the same situation 'see' the same thing?" If we have this ethics sense, why doesn't it act more like vision or touch or the other senses with which we are familiar? Shouldn't you and I *see* the same right thing?

If you and I look at an apple, and you say, "What a lovely red apple!" but I say, "What a lovely green apple!" there are several possible explanations. The way the light is shining on the apple could make it look red to one person and green to another. Or one of us might be sitting right next to the apple while the other is seeing it from a distance and just assuming that it is red. Or one of us may be color-blind.

We have a pretty good idea of how to settle this dispute. We would try to get the two individuals to view the apple from the same distance and perspective in broad daylight. If they still did not agree, we might make sure that the individuals are using the words "red" and "green" in the same way. To determine this, we might have them look at other red and green objects and see how they sort these things. Our final attempt at resolution would be to have the individuals tested for color blindness. We would not conclude that the apple is both red and green (unless the terms apply to only part of the apple) or that it has no color at all.

Most disputes about the colors of common objects can be settled in this way—but not all of them. It is said that Eskimos see more shades of snow than we do, so it might be hard for us to come to agreement with an Eskimo about a particular snowfall. And we are aware that there are optical illusions that trick the eye until we see the illusion from another perspective. Or we might be assessing the aesthetic merit of a picture with one viewer seeing beauty while the other sees only a jumble of asymmetric lines.

None of these disagreements about what we see leads us to question whether we can see. We try to address these discrepancies by changing the viewing conditions, checking the terminology, improving the lighting, or even by allowing for cultural differences (the snow).

When it comes to aesthetic judgment, the situation is closer to the situation with ethical judgment. Two observers may look at the same painting, e.g., Andy Warhol's famous Campbell's soup can, but disagree about whether they are seeing something aesthetically meritorious. This is parallel to the case in which two individuals have similar sympathetic and empathetic connections to a situation but cannot agree on the right course of action. The reason for this parallel is important.

The aesthetic sense is different from the five basic senses in just the way the ethics sense is different from sympathy, empathy, and the other traits related to this sense. Two people can look at the same picture and see the same thing but disagree about whether what they see has artistic merit. Similarly, two people can be similarly related to a situation in terms of sympathy and empathy but disagree as to whether an action is right. This underscores the fact that the ethics eye is separate and distinct from sympathy and empathy, although it is these qualities that allow it to function.

When there is a disagreement about the aesthetic merit of something, we can just agree to disagree. However, if you have a passion for a particular piece of art, you will seek the agreement of others. There are a number of ways you can do this. One way is to explain the techniques and challenges that went into creating the work of art. You can also explain the importance of the work of art in various social, cultural, historic, or artistic contexts. For example, we might point out that Andy Warhol's Campbell's soup can opened the door to a whole school of art or that his art revealed the beauty of everyday objects. We might also express the view that this piece of art was an expression of certain important themes that were present in our culture when it was created. We can even try to get people to look at the picture in different ways from different angles or in different lighting.

Warhol's Campbell's soup can is a wonderful example of the process of creating artistic agreement just because its artistic merit was much in question when it was created (and to some extent still is). The process of creating aesthetic agreement can be successful even if not everyone agrees. If enough people agree on the merit of a work of art, the work becomes valuable. There is no intrinsic price for a piece of art. Its price or economic value is based on what people are willing to pay—on an agreed upon price. Of course, a work of art can be expensive but not viewed as artistically meritorious. To establish the artistic merit of a piece of art, you have get at least some of those whose artistic judgment is respected—the art authorities—to agree with you.

In order to establish the aesthetic and monetary value of a work of art, you have to create agreement. Others must see the work of art in the way your aesthetic eye does. But you don't have to convince everyone. If you convince certain buyers, museums, or critics, you win.

It is also the case that part of the job with establishing the rightness of an action is to create agreement that the action is right. If you don't create agreement that the action is right, the action is unlikely to succeed, and you will be opposed or even punished for taking the action. But can you stop at getting just *some* of the folks to agree as you can with the aesthetic eye? The big difference between the ethics eye and the aesthetic eye is in the consequences. If someone doesn't like my painting of a soup can, the consequences are mainly to me. But an incorrect ethics judgment can change the direction of lives, organizations, even society itself. So while ethical disagreement does not show the absence of the ethics eye, it does point to an important conclusion:

If you want to be an effective ethics change agent, someone who makes an ethical difference, you have to be good at creating agreement.

Chapter Six

Ethical Action Means Ethical Agreement

"You can't agree that you can't agree."

—Mark Pastin

SITUATION #8 *Dead River*

Environmental issues are often ethically complex. When you judge the actions that governments and businesses took many years ago, there is a temptation to judge them by today's environmental standards. This can lead to conflicting, strongly held ethical judgments.

Such a situation occurred in the 1980s with respect to the so-called Dead Pigeon River, a river that flows through North Carolina and Tennessee. Several industrial companies, including several paper plants, had dumped their waste into the river over the years. The river was widely used for recreation until dioxin was discovered in the river and a related reservoir. Dioxin tends to settle at the bottom of a waterway or reservoir, with the consequence that trying to clean it up has the unintended effect of stirring it up, thus making matters worse. When dioxin was discovered in the Pigeon River, some environmentalists began calling it "The Dead Pigeon River." Many of the companies that had dumped dioxin into the river were no longer in business, and it was unlikely that any current employee or manager of the remaining companies was employed by them when the waste was dumped. To the environmentalists and some residents, it seemed obvious that the remaining companies were liable for the pollution. To the companies still operating, the environmentalists' position seemed unreasonable as no one currently involved with the companies had anything to do with releasing dioxin into the river. The Pigeon River gained even more notoriety in the 1988 U.S. presidential election when Al Gore was accused of running as an environmentalist while urging compromise on the cleanup of the Pigeon River.

Many employees of the companies along the Pigeon River felt that the current companies should not be held accountable for actions not known to be harmful when taken and taken long before the employees' association with the companies. As they saw it, it would be like arresting a child because his parent held up a store. This argument has its limits because companies are corporate persons within the law and their lifetime is unlimited. From a legal viewpoint, the "corporate person" who polluted the river years ago is the same "corporate person" who employs people today. Predictably, lawsuits ensued.

Predict the actual outcome of this situation and ask whether or not it is an ethical outcome. Compare your answers with the actual outcome at the end of this chapter.

We have spent considerable time talking about ethical disagreements. These disagreements are the main reason that ethics is discussed and they are the main reason I am called upon for ethics advice. In order to be effective in resolving ethical issues, we must learn how to build agreement out of disagreement. Agreement among parties is also important when it comes to doing the right thing, since it usually takes more than one person to take meaningful action. By agreement, I do not mean parties entering into a formal contract that might be called "the agreement." I mean that the parties to an ethical dispute come to share the same view—to be *in agreement*—as to the right course of action. In this chapter we build a better understanding of agreement in ethics so that we can employ an effective process for building ethical agreement in the following chapter.

How Much Agreement Is Enough?

How much agreement about ethical issues should we seek? How much agreement about an ethical issue is enough?

One of the problems with ethical issues is that people sometimes think that we should reach 100% agreement before taking an ethical position and acting on it. In other words, they believe that it must be possible to explain our actions so that *anyone*

89

would agree with them. And they take the absence of such universal agreement to preclude ethical action.

Universalists believe that paying a bribe to obtain business in a foreign country is either right or wrong. Allowing police officers to use drugs while working undercover is either right or wrong. Allowing a teenager who has become pregnant by her boyfriend to have an abortion is either right or wrong. These are issues on which it is hard to reach agreement among even a small group of individuals, let alone universal agreement. Since we are not good at getting 100% agreement on these things, we often conclude that we either do not have an innate ability to see what's right or, if we do, that it is not strong enough to guide us to ethical action.

People who are sincere about ethical change sometimes become discouraged just because reaching 100% agreement seems an impossible goal. When individuals committed to ethical change realize that it is nearly impossible to change some minds, they may give up on ethical change in favor of politics, law, or regulation. You don't need complete agreement to get a law passed or a regulation implemented. These seem like more likely ways to stop people from doing unethical things than trying to change enough minds. Unfortunately, we have tried the politics-law-regulation approach, and it has a produced a society choking on rules with little to show by way of ethical improvement. In fact, we rely so much on laws and regulations that we have forgotten that laws and regulations intended to produce ethical improvement must be based on some idea of what ethical improvement is.

Why do we require such complete agreement on ethics before we are willing to take a stand and act on it? Why is the idea that there are things on which people may never agree so troubling when it comes to ethics?

In the last chapter, we looked at analogies between ethics and art. To begin with, we have to admit that disagreements about ethics are more important than disagreements about aesthetics. Little in aesthetics is a matter of life and death. Despite this difference, there are important analogies between art and ethics.

In aesthetics, we often reach some level of consensus by first agreeing that there are somewhat reliable judges of aesthetic merit, such as museum curators, scholars of art, and established artists. When these individuals reach consensus that a work of art has artistic merit, we are somewhat inclined to go along with them. If agreement among these experts lasts centuries, we are even more inclined to concur in their judgment. But even if there is wide consensus, some of us may still disagree. I still see Bach as more of an engineer than a composer, no matter what the experts say. And there is no expectation that one hundred percent agreement is in the offing.

Even in science, complete agreement is rare. Mathematicians still do not agree about what Kurt Gödel proved (the famous "impossibility theorem") or whether it matters. Einstein's theory of relativity has stood the test of time only in the most general terms. We still do not know if the basic components of matter are particles, waves, strings, or some undreamed of sort of entity. None of this keeps us from using scientific conclusions to build things. That is why it is paradoxical that we set the bar so high on agreement for ethics. If the agreement we achieve in science is sufficient for action, why hold out for even more agreement in ethics?

CASE BY CASE AGREEMENT

While it is hard to agree on abstract ethical principles, it is much easier to achieve ethical agreement in a particular case or situation. In most of the cases considered to this point, the ethical approach was fairly obvious even if the way to achieve that approach was not obvious. We can now see the reason for this. If ethical agreement depends on an ethics sense, which is sharpest when the emotions of sympathy and empathy are engaged, this sense will be less effective in addressing broad issues with remote effects. The same goes for ethical thinking about the future. Our ethics sense, and its related emotions of sympathy and empathy, finds it harder to connect with imagined individuals in the future than with actual individuals here and now. Does our dependence on an ethics eye render us blind outside of a small circle?

Consider an ethical problem to see how this works.

One of today's hotly debated issues is whether we spend too much money trying to keep people alive for a little longer near the end of their lives. The argument is that there is only so much money for healthcare, so we should use these scarce dollars on younger people rather than wasting tens of millions of dollars on futile end-of-life care.

Let's see how this thinking plays out in a specific example.

Many readers were moved by Mitch Albom's book *Tuesdays With Morrie*.[10] The book is about the author's weekly meetings with an old professor, Morrie Schwarz, dying of ALS (Lou

Gehrig's disease). While Morrie is gradually losing control of his body as paralysis spreads from his limbs to his torso and beyond, he maintains a positive outlook. Even more, he makes real contributions to Mitch's life and the lives of the others who visit him. I do not want to retell the story except to say that is hard to read the book and not love and admire Morrie.

Suppose now that Morrie is your uncle and near the end of his life. But while he is still sentient and communicating, a doctor tells you that there is a powerful new drug that will not only keep Morrie alive for another year, but will also postpone further deterioration over that period. Morrie will meet the same end in a year that is just around the corner for him now. But he will get another year in his current state. The problem is that the drug is very expensive. Suppose for the sake of argument that Morrie's medical bills are being paid for by Medicare, which means that you and I are paying the bills.

So the question is whether or not it is worth the money to get the drug for Morrie, or at least give him the choice of taking the drug or not. (Some will argue that Morrie would decline the drug, but practical experience shows that end-of-life decisions are unpredictable.) It is widely believed that we are spending too much money on the last days of life and, without the drug, these are Morrie's last days. And, by any ordinary standard, it is not much of a life. Except for his ability to think and communicate, Morrie is paralyzed. Surely spending a lot of money to give him another year of the same is not the right thing to do.

Now Uncle Morrie is a pretty fine human being, and I would want him to have the choice of whether or not to take the life-extending drug. And I would respect his choice either way. If you gave me the argument about the wasteful use of resources, I would point out that we spend enough on cosmetics in a minute to pay for Morrie's drugs for a year. I believe that giving Uncle Morrie the option of another year of life is the right thing to do.

But what about the broader issue? Aren't we wasting precious dollars at the end of life for no good reason? I think it is perfectly possible to side with me on Morrie and still hold the basic view that we are overspending on end-of-life care. This appears to be an inconsistency and I think it is. One of the revelations of life as an ethics advisor is how little influence abstract principles have when those you know are involved. What is not clear is whether we should sacrifice Morrie to save the principle.

How can we reconcile what our moral sense tells us in a particular case, such as Morrie's, with a conflicting general opinion on end-of-life care? Do we reason that since the principle is logical, we shouldn't let our emotions rule our thinking? Or do we see that the general principle is only a good one if it addresses particular cases correctly? Isn't that what a sound general principle is supposed to do?

If ethical opinions are like other opinions based on our senses, our general opinion on end-of-life spending should be based on what our ethics sense tells us in particular cases. I am confident that many of you would reach the same conclusion as I have in the case of Morrie, at least if you had gotten to know Morrie. If we trust our ethics sense in the case of Morrie, even if it is only a single case, then we have to modify our view on the wastefulness of end-of-life care. The operation of the moral sense in this case requires a qualification of today's mantra of "let the nearly dead die." A more accurate principle is that we should let the nearly dead die *if that is their choice*. This is a general principle we can stand by no matter how we judge Morrie's case.

But if we leave it up to the dying and their families to decide their own willingness to die, aren't we going to waste a lot of money? This depends on the questionable assumption that if we save money on end-of-life care the very same money will be better spent on younger individuals who are sick. But can we conclude that it won't be spent on highway repairs, pork belly projects, and fat pensions for members of Congress? Money doesn't travel in a straight line from one use to another.

FROM THE SPECIFIC TO THE GENERAL

The point of this hypothetical case about Morrie is not to convince you of my view on end-of-life spending. Rather, this case, whether or not you agree with me, shows how the conclusions we draw in specific cases using our ethics sense drive our broader ethical judgment.

Rather than surrendering our ethical insights in particular cases to broader principles and policy concerns, it is the principles and policy concerns that should be informed by application of the ethics sense in the situations that make up our lives.

Compare this to the way we learn in science. Suppose an ornithologist proposes a genetically sound theory according to which all swans are white. No matter how compelling this theory, if we observe but one black swan, the theory has to go.

Or consider today's physics. Physics consists of a host of scientific hypotheses about how the world works. The edifice of physics reflects the work of some of the greatest minds the world has known. But if this great edifice of physics predicts that my pencil will fly into the sky as opposed to falling on the floor when I drop it, something in that physics has to go. Of course, should my pencil begin to fly we would try all sorts of explanations within that physics to try to explain my observation of a flying pencil. But if there is no good explanation, such as that I am hallucinating, then that one observation—whether of one black swan or one flying pencil—is enough to show a defect in physics.

Perhaps my flying pencil might be some sort of quantum phenomenon. Quantum physics tells us that there is randomness in the universe, at least at the subatomic level, so you may think that my pencil flying away is a random event that we should just write off. But that is not how quantum physics works. In fact, quantum physics goes to great lengths to explain why *we never do see random events* at the macro level of ordinary experience. Quantum physics makes the same predictions about our day-to-day observations as high school physics does. Quantum physics, just like plain old high school physics, predicts that my pencil will hit the floor. If the pencil flies away, quantum physics is in as much trouble as high school physics.

Observation through the senses tests theories and not the other way around. If science tells me my Weber grill is a porpoise, it is wrong. And the same is true in ethics; *the general is tested by the specific*. Understanding this is the key to the process of building ethical agreement. The difference is that in science we believe that our senses are generally trustworthy. There is no way to prove that our senses are trustworthy except by trusting our senses. And the same is true in ethics. Our ethics sense is trustworthy in its observations of particular situations, at least if we are willing to trust it.

LESSONS ON AGREEMENT

We have learned two things about agreement and disagreement in ethics.

The first is that *we need not reach agreement with everyone to have enough agreement to trust the ethics eye* and act on what it shows. For the ethics eye to work, we need to use it responsibly by ensuring that we make every effort to understand the ground rules, interests, and perspectives of others. We need to be sure that we have looked at a situation carefully enough that our empathetic and sympathetic reactions to the situation fully engage our ethics eye. There will always be others who do not take the trouble to create conditions in which the ethics eye can be trusted. Ideally, we would get everyone to look at the situation under conditions that focus their ethics eyes. But it is not realistic to expect this in every case.

The second thing we have learned is that settling conflicts about general ethical principles is not a matter of arguing about the principles. *It is a matter of testing the principles against what we see in particular cases.* In most of the cases reviewed in *Make an Ethical Difference,* seeing the right course of action has not been a problem, even if pursuing that course of action is. Even when we cannot see what is right immediately, we can use tools to sharpen the ethics eye and bring us closer to seeing what is right. *When we want to resolve differences about ethical principles, we should start with specific cases, cases in which the ethics eye is most acute, and proceed from these cases to general principles on which we can agree.*

We shall see in the next chapter that if we set realistic expectations about the extent to which people can agree on ethical situations, we can use the tools developed for our own ethical insight to produce agreement with others. An organized process incorporating these tools will help us move from seeing what is right in specific cases to agreement with others about both cases and principles. An agreement with others is often what allows us to make an ethical difference.

SITUATION #8 *Dead River (continued)*

The problem in the Dead River case is that holding the companies accountable today for what they did when they were run by different people with different employees punishes current managers, employees, and shareholders for deeds in which they had no part. On the other hand, if the companies are not held accountable, the people who live along the river will be punished for something they did not do, and companies will escape responsibility for their actions merely by outliving them. This dispute actually went to trial with the sides taking the above stances. A mistrial was declared. It became evident to the parties to this dispute that settling matters in court would serve no one's purpose. This meant that the parties themselves had to reach agreement, which, to the surprise of many, they did. Because the ground rules of the two sides could not be brought into agreement, the two sides took the process to the next step, which is to look at the interests involved. The companies agreed to pay those who lived along the river a significant amount. While this amount was less than it would take to clean up the dioxin, it was enough to significantly help those affected by it. Even though there was no agreement on ground rules, it was possible to achieve agreement based on interests.

This is often the kind of agreement on ethical issues you can achieve. *You have to allow for this kind of ethical agreement if you want to make an ethical difference in the real world.* It may not please the philosophers and pundits, but it serves as the basis for taking action.

Interlude: Ethics Across Cultures

One of the biggest red herrings in ethics is that we cannot reach enough agreement in ethics to have firm views because of irresolvable differences among cultures. This is much like saying that because there are cultures in which scientific method is not respected, we cannot arrive at truth in science. I do not see a growing doubt in science caused by the persistence of voodoo. In the case of science, we know this is baloney. Why do we maintain our confidence in science despite cultural differences? Because science helps predict what our senses recognize as facts.

For some reason, people give more weight to cultural differences when it comes to ethics. For example, when I was in college I was told that we view obligations to the elderly differently than some Eskimos, who will send the old off into the frozen tundra to die in peace. But I have witnessed healthcare delivered in Eskimo villages. When their options for the care of the elderly are similar to ours, they make the same healthcare decisions we do.

I have done business on five continents, not only as an ethics advisor but also as a general business consultant. I have yet to find a place in which honesty is not valued. I was in Japan shortly after the Lockheed bribery scandal broke. (See Chapter Nine for more on the Lockheed bribery scandal.) It was alleged as part of the scandal that various members of the Diet and Japan's Prime Minister were involved in taking bribes. I have been told many times that this was culturally acceptable in Japan. But why then did Prime Minister Tanaka and many members of the Diet resign in disgrace?

Just because ordinary people cannot *prevent* their leaders from taking bribes does not mean that bribery is acceptable. We often hear the same story with respect to Mexico, that bribery is acceptable there. But the ordinary Mexican citizens I know are as disgusted as anyone over the corruption in their society.

The ethics eye is a human trait not a cultural artifact. There are no cultures in which there is no ability to sympathize or empathize, the triggers to the ethics sense, and none in which there is no distinction between right and wrong. The distinction between right and wrong may be different than ours, but it exists. This means that the tools we use to sharpen the ethics eye and to create ethical agreement have a chance of producing ethical agreement across cultures. When we are too quick to write off ethical disagreements as cultural artifacts, we lose the possibility of using our ethics sense to achieve insight and agreement. Maybe some cultural differences are so deep that we cannot expect ethical agreement. But shouldn't we at least try? I am not suggesting that we force others to follow our ethics. I am suggesting that we try to find common ground in ethics even at the risk of changing our own views.

What happened on the issue of ethics and culture is that for many years we simply assumed that our ethical viewpoint was *the* ethical viewpoint. When anthropologists began to probe other cultures, they correctly found this attitude to be arrogant and one-sided. But the factors that cause different people in different cultures to disagree are often the same factors that cause people *within a culture* to disagree. I think the extent to which there are irresolvable ethical differences among cultures is often overestimated as a sort of penance for our past arrogance. Once we recognize our ethics sense, and develop tools to sharpen it, there is no reason not to seek ethical agreement within and across cultures.

Chapter Seven

Yes, We Can Agree on Ethics

"Some great minds think alike."

—Mark Pastin

SITUATION #9 *Private Interests*

The CEO of a publicly traded company was grappling with the following problem. The company developed software for business applications and had a history of consistent earnings. The model for selling the company's software was that the software would be provided to value-added resellers who then sold the software to customers along with a service and support package. A unit of the software package was considered sold when the reseller sold the unit to a customer. The reseller had the right to return units to the company if they had not sold before an updated edition appeared.

The problem was that one iteration of the product was a dud and units were coming back in volume. There was a new version available that promised to correct the problems and it was being shipped to the resellers. However, it would be months before there were new sales. There was a risk that the company would lose its credit line and be forced into bankruptcy in the interim.

The Chief Financial Officer of the company advised the CEO that a slight change in accounting practices, still within generally accepted accounting principles, could save the day. While it was a matter of some complexity, the basic idea was to count units as sold when they were delivered to the reseller rather than when the reseller sold the units to a customer. If sales were slow, as in the current circumstance, they could put a lot of product in the sales channels that would count as sold. (This practice is called "stuffing the channels.") Since resellers still had the right to return products, sales would be adjusted by the historical return rate, which, until recently, was quite low. This strategy would yield good sales numbers while the new generation of products brought sales up to speed. The company would show consistent sales, its credit line would be intact, and, before anyone had a chance to object, the company would be back in good shape.

The CEO was intrigued by this idea especially since the company's external auditors signed off on the change in accounting practices. All of this could be included in a Securities and Exchange Commission filing that was unlikely to attract attention. And even if there were objections, they would take time. The company would be back on its feet by then and could adjust past earnings accordingly.

Would it be wrong for the CEO to make this change in accounting practices? Use the process described in this chapter to see if you and the CEO can see eye to eye on this issue.

We already have the tools needed to pursue ethical agreement. So far we have applied these tools to sharpen our own ability to see what is right. What we lack is a systematic process by which these tools can help us reach agreement *with others.* We are not seeking agreement by force or through apathy. *We seek a situation in which what I see as right is also what you see as right.* The importance of reaching ethical agreement cannot be overestimated. Most ethical issues require the effort of more than one person to result in ethical action. This is where agreement comes in. When you have agreement with others, you have a better chance of taking actions that make an ethical difference.

If you and I disagree about ethics, there are three ways to reach agreement. You change your mind. I change my mind. Or we both change our minds. When you undertake a sincere process of seeking ethical agreement, two of the three options for doing so involve changing your mind. You have to accept at the outset that your ethical perspective may be the one that changes in the process of seeking ethical agreement.

It is often difficult to admit that you may be the one who is wrong about an ethical issue. It is especially hard to admit that you may be wrong if you have gone to the trouble to consider the ground rules, the interests, the facts, and the perspectives of others. Why change your mind to reach agreement with others who have not done much to arrive at their position?

This is the hardest part of using the ethics eye. *In order to reach agreement about ethics, you have to put your own position on the line.* When others disagree and you are convinced you are right, you have to work toward agreement by getting them to sharpen their ethics eye. You typically have to do this without saying, "I have gone to great trouble to understand this matter and I now need you to see the situation clearly." This will not lead anyone to give your viewpoint a chance. You have to lead others to engage their ethics eyes without assuming a position of superiority. Don't forget that your own ethics eye may be engaged by the process in ways you don't expect. Just as you are trying to influence the ethics sense of others, they may be trying to influence you. You may end up losing this tug of war!

PUT YOUR VIEW ON THE LINE

When we are trying to work out an ethical disagreement, we seek a situation in which your innate ethics sense and my innate ethics sense see the same course of action as right. I call the process for reaching ethical agreement the "Convergence Process," since we are trying to get our ethics eyes to converge on one view of a situation.

Just because you and I reach agreement does not mean that we have found *the* right position. Even if you and I are the only two individuals contemplating an ethical situation, the fact that we agree does not mean that others would agree. And, even if we build wide consensus around our viewpoint, it is not a sure thing that we are right. Agreement in ethics is exactly like agreement in science or art in that even a wide consensus does not guarantee truth. There is always the possibility of revision based on what our senses—in this case our ethics sense—tell us. The fact that we may always need to revise our views is not, however, reason to lose trust in the whole process of seeking truth.

The goal in ethics is not purity of theory or elegance of viewpoint. The goal is to do the right thing. When someone with a far-out view disagrees with me, I may find this theoretically interesting. But if you and I need to decide on a course of action, there typically is not time to consider every remote possibility. Because ethics is about the rightness of what we do, the most important step is to gain the agreement of those who will take the action and those who will be affected it. If the individuals taking the action and the individuals affected by the action see merit in what we are doing, we have satisfied the most important audiences.

Let's see how the Convergence Process works through a situation in which you and I are trying to reach agreement on the right thing to do. This is a modest example in that we seek the agreement of only two individuals. But, even if the scope of agreement is limited, the process by which we reach agreement is the same as that appropriate to more complex situations.

SAFE AT ANY SPEED?

Suppose you and I work for a major car manufacturer in the product development area. It is our job to decide whether to move a particular design, code-named the "BeastMobile," into production. The BeastMobile has all the modern safety features—and a huge power-to-weight ratio. It is a very fast car.

Your position is that there is a public demand for very fast cars, even if these cars are seldom used at their potential. And even though these cars cannot legally be used to full potential on public roads, they can be raced at a racetrack. And the fact that the car would be at home at a racetrack makes the car more attractive to owners who would never consider going to a racetrack to race their own car. They just want the buzz of going from 0 to 60 miles per hour in a few seconds. And they want others to know that they could go very fast if they wanted to. We are selling image rather than mechanics.

My position is that there is no logical reason to produce a car capable of traveling twice the highest legal speed limit. Even if the BeastMobile were 100% safe when used appropriately, such vehicles are not always used appropriately. They are used when people are on ego trips, drunk or stoned, and while they are texting. And when they are used inappropriately, these cars are dangerous not only to their drivers and passengers, but also to anyone else on or near the road. My position is that a responsible manufacturer would not sell the BeastMobile.

The disagreement we are having over the BeastMobile occurs every day in businesses across the world. I have witnessed this very pattern of reasoning encompassing products as diverse as nuclear reactors and the milk we buy in the grocery store. I was once in the middle of a debate about how safe a children's car seat has to be before it can be sold. The truth is that we are selling and buying car seats that could be improved upon. How safe does the milk in the grocery store have to be in order to be sold? Spend enough money on the production and distribution process and you can almost entirely eliminate the possibility of salmonella in milk. But people shop for car seats and milk based partly on price and not on safety alone.

The issues at the core of these decisions are ethical. How much safety has to be built into a product for it to be responsibly sold? How much risk should consumers be allowed to impose on themselves?

We mostly try to hide from the ethical issues involved in these cases. When a car seat malfunctions, resulting in the death of a child, the manufacturer pretends that the seat could not have been made safer. But it could have been. The critic pretends that the manufacturer was only concerned with cost—and, presumably, that customers were not concerned with price. But consumers will only pay so much for safety. By refusing to address the ethical issues forthrightly, we create a feeding frenzy for the plaintiff's attorneys and the media.

One of the most common ways of ducking the ethical issues involved in these situations is to fall back on whether a product meets government safety standards. When companies are trying to figure out how risky a product they can sell, they often draw the line at whether the product can be legally made and sold. As if one should do anything that is legal. This stance makes the government the final arbiter of consumer safety. The inconsistency of this position becomes apparent when the very same companies fight government safety standards on the grounds that consumers should be able to decide for themselves—a position that makes no sense if you concede the role of protector of public safety to the government. I am not denying that government standards play a legitimate role. But you have to decide if you can ethically make and sell a product before considering whether it satisfies government regulations. Just because you can legally make a hand grenade usable by ten-year-olds is not a reason to make or sell it.

THE CONVERGENCE PROCESS

Your (hypothetical) ethics eye and mine disagree when focused on selling the BeastMobile. *The first step in trying to resolve an ethical disagreement is to be sure the parties to the disagreement are looking at the same facts.* You may believe that the Beast-Mobile is so well designed and incorporates so many safety features that it is only dangerous if a driver is seriously crazy or incompetent. And any car, high-powered or not, is dangerous when operated by a seriously crazy and/or incompetent driver.

When I look at the BeastMobile, I see a car that has so much power that some drivers will be unable to resist testing its limits. And if they do so, all the safety features in the world won't protect them.

We disagree about the facts. We we are looking at the same situation but seeing it differently partly because of differing factual assumptions. There is no guarantee that we will ever agree on the facts, but at least we know what we have to do to reach agreement. We have to agree on a methodology for settling the facts and be prepared to accept the outcome of applying that methodology. I am the first to admit that because of our emotional connection to cars, especially fast cars, it may be hard to settle the facts. But we could if we wanted to.

The BeastMobile situation shows us the first step in the process of reaching ethical agreement.

Step #1

Face the facts. Bring any facts on which the parties disagree to the surface and attempt to resolve these factual disagreements impartially. When you are having trouble agreeing on the facts, try to reach agreement on a method for settling the facts and apply this method. Remember that you may have to revisit the facts once you have considered the ground rules, interests, and perspectives of those affected.

The factual issues relevant to our disagreement about the BeastMobile include: How dangerous is the BeastMobile? What percentage of BeastMobile owners will drive incompetently or irresponsibly? If the BeastMobile is used incompetently or irresponsibly, how likely is an accident? If there is an accident, who is likely to be hurt, only the driver or are others likely to be injured? If the BeastMobile is not brought to market, will similar cars be available to consumers? Is the BeastMobile safer or less safe than these other cars? Is it possible to produce and sell the BeastMobile within existing laws and regulations?

It is possible that once we answer these questions of fact, we will no longer disagree. But I don't think so. Our disagreement depends on differences between our ground rules and not just the facts. In other words, even if we agree on the risk posed by the BeastMobile, you and I would still differ on whether consumers should be *allowed* to bear that risk.

When *facing the facts* fails to bring convergence to our ethics eyes, the next step is to *read the ground rules.*

Step #2

In order to see if an ethical disagreement is about ground rules, identify the ground rules of the parties to the disagreement. Try *reading the ground rules* common to all parties as well as those that may be the source of the disagreement. When the parties to the disagreement see the ground rules on which they agree, this may allow agreement on the case at hand. When the parties to the disagreement see the ground rules on which they disagree, there may be room for change on one or all sides.

Our disagreement over the BeastMobile is partly about ground rules. My ground rules say, "A company should not sell products that pose significant risks to consumers or others associated with the product." Your ground rules say, "Consumers are entitled to buy risky products provided that the risks have been minimized and the consumer has been informed of them." And, while we could seek common ground rules, I doubt that either of us would compromise on the ground rules at the core of this disagreement.

Another reason we may have reached a stalemate is that I have emphasized the risks to people who are *not* buyers of the BeastMobile. And gaining the buyer's acceptance of the risks associated with the BeastMobile does not gain the consent of others exposed to the risks. The issue goes beyond our ground rules concerning consumer protection.

By introducing *non*-consumers who may be injured by the BeastMobile, I have introduced a whole new set of interests into our disagreement.

Step #3

If the facts and ground rules don't resolve an ethical disagreement, *find the interests* involved in the situation. In addition to *finding the interests* of the parties to the disagreement, *find the interests* of the others who may be affected by the decision. To ensure coverage of interests, go beyond finding the interests to considering them collectively. Use the *global benefit approach* to see if there is agreement over what course of action will produce the greatest balance of benefit over harm.

The BeastMobile situation, like most significant business situations, involves many interests. Obvious interests include those of the company producing BeastMobiles and those of the consumers purchasing them. The range of related interests explodes to include families of consumers, employees of the company, those who will pay for potential healthcare consequences, competitors of the company, regulators, insurers, other users of public streets, and more. If we look at this web of interests through the *global benefit approach*, we can make some progress.

If we assume that there is consumer demand for very fast cars, we can safely assume that if we don't produce the Beast-Mobile, someone else will produce and sell such a car, potentially without all of the safety features of the BeastMobile. In fact, the greatest good may be served if we produce the BeastMobile, since competitors may be forced to match our safety features, thereby increasing the safety of very fast cars as a class. This line of reasoning is sufficient to move me toward producing the BeastMobile, but there is one more aspect to consider. Even if the BeastMobile passes the *global benefit approach,* we have to consider the impact of the BeastMobile on others, and not just as part of the *global benefit approach* equation.

Step #4

If you are unable reach agreement based on facts, ground rules, and interests, make your focus increasingly specific. *Stand in the shoes* of others who may be critically affected by the decision. To the extent possible, make these potentially affected parties participants in your deliberations.

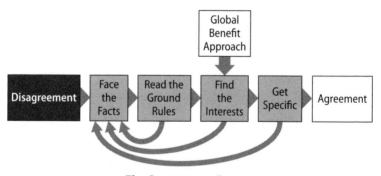

The Convergence Process

Since you favor the BeastMobile, you would invite participation by the BeastMobile's designers, the workers who will be employed producing and selling it, and those involved in safety testing the vehicle. You want me to see those who will benefit from the BeastMobile's production. You also want me to see that those charged with safety testing the BeastMobile were conscientious in ensuring that it is as safe as possible. In short, you want me to see that the BeastMobile will make a positive difference to many individuals.

Since I am opposed to the BeastMobile, I might invite the participation of some of the people who buy and often misuse "ego" cars. I might even ask you to talk to the former owner of a Ferrari or Lamborghini who was seriously injured in an accident. My job is to make the risks of producing the BeastMobile concrete as opposed to being viewed in terms of abstract probabilities.

Since our consideration of the BeastMobile is hypothetical, there is no way to know whether this process would yield agreement on the ethics of producing and selling the BeastMobile. I have participated in many decisions of this kind and, on that basis, I would predict agreement. This is partly because we have to reach agreement to move forward in any direction.

Here is how I think it would turn out.

My thinking: The fact that someone else will make very fast cars, whether or not we do, does not relieve us of responsibility for the BeastMobile. But it does prove that there will be such cars no matter what we do. So I would go along with selling the BeastMobile on certain conditions. The car should include a mechanism to warn drivers of misuse. I would verify that we have made the car as safe as possible and lobby for a speed moderator that could be disabled only under test or track conditions. Most importantly, I would urge the company to lead an effort to stop the production of all cars whose power exceeds any legitimate use.

You, I think, would agree with me up to a point. You would argue that we cannot so disable the car that consumers would no longer consider it a legitimate "supercar." I believe you would meet me half way on the issue of speed moderators. I doubt that we would have instant success in restricting supercars without speed monitors to the track.

In the real world, the terms of ethical agreement typically do not make for banner headlines and moving stump speeches. Doing what one considers right without seeking ethical agreement is more likely to thwart than accomplish your ethical objectives. Most ethically significant actions require the participation of more than one person.

If the goal is to act ethically, seeking agreement is essential. A "no compromise" approach is the right approach if you want to feel good and have others notice you, while accomplishing little. On the other hand, the process of ethical agreement is more likely to lead to the actions that make an ethical difference.

SITUATION #9 *Private Interests (continued)*

Let's return to our struggling software company. When you are the leader of a public company, your every action affects an array of interests. If the CEO in this situation wants to protect the interests of the company's employees, including its executives, he will change accounting practices with as little notice as possible. There is also a self-interested reason for the CEO to take this approach. Most CEOs are paid partly in stock. The CEO can hedge his personal bets by gradually selling some of his stock while the new version of the software enters the market. Of course, trades made under these conditions are both ethically and legally suspect.

However, changing accounting practices in this way is clearly intended to deceive the company's investors and regulators, not to mention its resellers, vendors, and other business partners. If there were no intention to deceive, the change in accounting practices could be openly announced. Of course, were it openly announced, it would serve no purpose, since everyone would see the company's dire financial circumstances. On the other hand, if the company changes accounting practices with little fanfare and the company goes on to prosper, this deceit will get little attention.

CEOs in save-the-company mode are dangerous. CEOs in this mode can justify almost any action on the premise that the ultimate good of many will be served. When I looked at this situation with the CEO, I encouraged him to believe that he could pull the company through while being candid about his actions. In essence, my argument was that an effective CEO would not have to resort to subterfuge. When it seemed that this approach was not working, I began to suspect that the new products might not be much better than their predecessors. If this were true, the deceptive accounting practices would hurt everyone when the collapse finally happened. Only the CEO and top company leadership might benefit by dumping their holdings before the public realized that the accounting change masked poor performance.

In the end, this CEO decided to be up front about the change in accounting practices, while pointing out that many other high-tech firms already used this approach. While the next generation of products was only moderately successful, the CEO was able to keep the company going on the strength of his reputation for leading struggling companies. His candor with the markets didn't hurt. Did the CEO take this approach because he considered it the right thing to do? Or did he take it out of fear of the consequences of being secretive?

When your goal is to make an ethical difference, sometime you just have to be satisfied with agreement on a good outcome, no matter the motives precipitating that agreement.

Interlude: The Use of Force

I was once hired by an academic institution to turn around a department mired in mediocrity. I promptly concluded that the department was mediocre mainly because it liked being mediocre. The members of the department did not want to do the necessary work to improve. There was, however, one young member of the department who was an all-around champion—book accepted by a major publisher, articles in prestigious journals, super teaching evaluations, and a nice person as well.

Academia works on a strange version of peer evaluation according to which everyone superior to you in rank votes on whether you are retained, promoted, and tenured. In this case, it meant that a young faculty member with a record of excellence would be judged by the higher ranking mediocrities. I called a meeting to order where the main item of business was whether or not this individual would be retained and promoted. The case appeared to be open-and-shut, but we had the usual conversation just to uphold the process. Someone said, "I don't like the fact that she acts like she is better than us." I had to stifle a smile at that one. Another faculty member said, "She is not a team player and that should count for something." This was followed by a comment from the least competent member of the department: "What do you expect—she's a Jew?" I felt my fury rise at least partly because I thought that I had been a fool to take on improving this sorry lot. At that point I said, "I am calling for a vote." The members of the department knew that I was daring them to vote me down. I won on a 19 to 1 (the bigot) vote, for retention and promotion of the young faculty member. I did not seek agreement; I used power to get my way.

It is always better to seek ethical agreement than to act despite a lack of agreement. But agreement is not always within practical reach. I was not going to change the bigot's mind. You cannot take the position that you will only act on what your ethics eye tells you if your ethics eye and the ethics eyes of all others completely converge. When you have to act without agreement, it is always a good idea to check what your ethics eye is telling you. Ask yourself if the reason that agreement cannot be reached is because you have failed to consider certain ground rules, interests, or viewpoints. But the goal of seeing what is right is to be empowered to *do* what you see as right. And that sometimes means acting on your own ethics sense without the agreement of others.

Chapter Eight

A Few Words about Big Issues

"An issue is as big as the lie you can tell about it."

—unattributed

SITUATION #10   *Easy Conscience*

A terminal patient is in great pain but, with the concurrence of his family, refuses, for religious reasons, to allow the plug (on further therapeutic treatment) to be pulled. However, the patient requests that everything be done to reduce the pain to the maximum possible extent. The patient's physicians explain that the pain can be reduced and almost eliminated, but at the expense of the patient's consciousness and, imminently, his life. The patient and the patient's family find this consequence acceptable. The physicians, however, wonder if they are participating in an assisted suicide.

If you were called into this situation, what advice would you give to the physician in charge and the family members? Would your advice depend on your general views concerning euthanasia? Compare your advice to the advice actually given in this case at the end of the chapter.

You may wonder if we are ever going to tackle the "big issues" in ethics. These issues include abortion, environmental concerns, the ethics of war, euthanasia, international bribery, and genetic engineering, among others. While our focus is on the day-to-day decisions we make in our work and private lives, shouldn't ethics tools work on the larger issues of ethical concern, too? Shouldn't we seek to make an ethical difference on the larger stage, as well?

One problem with the big issues is that posing them as big issues presupposes that there are big answers. When we assume that there are big answers, we tend to embody those big answers in laws and regulations that force one ethical viewpoint on everyone. While this may sometimes be necessary, it is always better if a law or regulation embodies an ethical consensus. Since getting laws and regulations passed is a matter of political power—as opposed to ethical reasoning—there is always the chance that the viewpoint being ignored is the correct one.

While we shall address three big issues—euthanasia, international bribery, and healthcare ethics—in this and the next two chapters, our focus is on the *process* by which our ethics sense enables us to address big issues. We will see how our tools for ethical decision making can help us with broader issues of ethical concern.

BOTTOM UP BEATS TOP DOWN

We know that the ethics eye works best in situations in which our human reactions of empathy and sympathy are triggered. In this regard, the ethics eye is like the other senses that lose acuity as their object becomes more distant. It has taken centuries to build the body of knowledge that exists today based on observations made with the five senses. The body of knowledge in ethics has not grown commensurately. This is partly because we have failed to recognize the importance of the data provided by our innate ethics sense. By not building a body of knowledge based on our ethics sense, we have allowed ideologues to monopolize the ethical conversation. Ideologues fear the intrusion of independent, unbiased evidence. It is not too far-fetched to say that while science has advanced immeasurably since the "dark ages," our ethical knowledge has grown comparatively little.

But if this is true, will we ever be able to understand big issues and fundamental ground rules? What is the right starting place?

The big issues in ethics are often approached in an upside-down manner. When we think about the issue of abortion, as an example, we tend to think that the answer lies in some principle or principles that will resolve the issue decisively in every case. Perhaps a principle about the sanctity of all life or, alternatively, a principle about every person's right to self-determination. These principles tend to be vague and hard to apply in actual situations unless the individual is only using principles to rationalize what they have already decided. We often try to start with the principle and make everything fit. This would be like starting with the principles of quantum mechanics and trying to cook dinner based on them.

This is why we sometimes see advocates of an issue of public importance, whether it is abortion, gay marriage, or water boarding, take one position in their public pronouncements and quite another position when it comes to their private lives. When ideologies are up against the ethics eye operating at close range, ideologies lose their luster.

Our strategy here has been the opposite. Our strategy has been to work from specific situations toward principles. This strategy is based not only on the working of the ethics eye, but more generally on the way knowledge *in any field* grows. It would have been foolish to speculate about movement at the periphery of the universe if we had not tracked the orbits of the main planets. But in ethics, people want to jump from a single case to bold generalizations about how *everyone* should *act all of the time.* That is why we so often see heated arguments about the big ethical issues, with little progress to show for the effort.

There is surely a better way to build our ethical knowledge.

One Big Issue

Let's start by tackling a "big issue," euthanasia, on which there is a significant difference of opinion. People tend to have dug in their heels on issues such as abortion, water boarding, or gay marriage. It is hard to look rationally at an issue when commitment to a position is so strong that it beats back any challenges.

Views on euthanasia are not quite as entrenched, and by examining euthanasia, we will develop a strategy for approaching even the most divisive ethical issues.

The Morrie Schwarz issue discussed earlier is a related but different issue. In that case, we were testing our views on the use of medical resources at or near the end of life. Here we are concerned with the extent to which a person should be allowed to determine when to end her own life.

Some of my more recent work has been in the area of medical ethics, an area in which you often encounter life and death issues. People tend to be set in their viewpoint on these issues until they confront a situation that requires a personal decision. Today we have the odd situation in the United States that euthanasia is banned in most states even though many people believe euthanasia is ethically permissible or even ethically indicated in some cases.

Despite the laws outlawing euthanasia, euthanasia is an everyday occurrence. While there are few practitioners of what might be called "active euthanasia" of the kind practiced by Jack Kevorkian, the same outcome is regularly achieved by allowing patients to dehydrate, removing them from life support, or subjecting them to such high levels of pain killers that the patient essentially dies of anesthesia.

There is a practical reason for allowing a gap between euthanasia laws and actual practice. The practical reason for making euthanasia illegal is the fear that if that euthanasia is legalized there will be too much pressure to end lives while there is still a chance of recovery. There is so much pressure today not to be accused of wasting medical resources that this is a reasonable concern. In addition to social pressure to end lives, many families suffer greatly in the final years of their relatives' lives, and there is a fear that they might give up on a patient to order to save *themselves* further suffering. And some families might favor euthanasia to keep an estate from being squandered. While this is an ugly motivation, anyone who does what I do knows that it is not uncommon.

On the other side of this issue, there are many cases in which a patient has nothing to look forward to except unbearable pain and semiconsciousness due to painkillers. Some patients survive a long time in this "in between" state even though it is apparent to all that this is not a life the patient would choose to live. Faced with this situation, I have seen even those with a profound religious objection to euthanasia change their mind to stop the patient's suffering.

People have struggled so hard with these issues that there are even new categories of treatment designed to subvert anti-euthanasia laws. For example, when a patient no longer wants to live, it is permissible to ask him if he would like extreme measures to prevent further pain. Even though everyone knows that the patient will become unconscious and never regain consciousness before death, the patient has not been asked outright to choose to end his life. What we are talking about here is sometimes called "total euthanasia," since the medications used to reduce pain also kill the patient. The legality of total anesthesia is complex since much depends on the intentions of those ordering the painkillers, as opposed to any written or observable fact.

Anyone involved in end-of-life decisions knows how grueling and unique each situation is. Things are simpler when the patient has expressed her wishes, preferably in writing. Even then, you have to ask whether the patient meant what she wrote and whether she would make the same choices today. When you are using your ethics sense in such situations, you have to consider the ground rules (would the patient object to euthanasia on religious grounds) and interests (interests of patient versus interests of family and caregivers). You also have to stand in the shoes of the patient and ask what you would want were you in his circumstances. Finally, you have to be very specific to the facts and conditions at hand. If you use our tools to sharpen the ethics eye, it is likely that you will call some situations one way and other situations the other way. And each decision may be correct in the specific circumstances in which it is made.

ASK THE RIGHT QUESTION

How do we generalize from this diversity of outcomes to address the question of whether euthanasia is right or wrong? The closer you get to actual cases, you more you believe that there just isn't an overall right or wrong answer. In fact, we may be asking the wrong question when we ask whether or not euthanasia is ethical. The question we might ask instead is "*Who* should make decisions about whether euthanasia is right or wrong in particular situations?" Trying to force a single answer on all cases just leads us to where we are today, which is finding ways to circumvent laws that assume there is a single answer.

From our discussion of the ethics eye, you may conclude, as I have, that the decision about a particular situation should be made, with certain protective conditions, by those closest to it. A decision about euthanasia in a particular case is ideally suited to the proper use of the ethics eye. The protective conditions include trying to honor the patient's wishes if they have been expressed. It should also be understood that various parties to the decision may have interests other than those of the patient. These interests need to surface and be discussed. Finally, we should use our knowledge of the patient to stand in his or her shoes.

The case of euthanasia also shows that we sometime seek an overall principle or a law as a way of avoiding the challenges of making good choices in difficult situations. Instead of fully engaging the ethics eye, we seek an escape that leaves us with no decision to make.

What if we looked at other big ethical issues in this way? Would we always conclude that a general principle is likely to be flawed when viewed through the specific cases to which it applies? The reasoned answer is that in some cases, we will find general principles that give guidance in specific cases. But I suspect that in many other cases, the principles typically applied cannot be supported. Why is this?

Urged on by philosophers and theologians, we have always tried to start with principles and make our ethics sense conform to these principles. This is exactly how science was done in the Middle Ages when even the principles by which the physical world works were derived from theological sources. Even when confronted with situations in which science based on religious dogma was plain wrong, most thinkers clung to the principles. In science, we have moved beyond this way of thinking. In science, the experiment and its related observations rule. But in ethics, our thinking follows the same pattern it followed in the Middle Ages, that is, starting with principles that are "given" or "revealed" and forcing the cases to fit. We are early in the process of recognizing our ethics sense and using it to guide us to principles—and not the other way around.

Interlude: Ethics and Markets

The idea that ethical principles should be derived from the use of the ethics eye in individual cases has a close relationship to the theory of the market, specifically, to the theory of the consumer and the firm. In essence, the theory of the market says that allowing markets to function with consumers freely choosing among products provides the *best information* for business and economic planning. Instead of planning centrally, where there is mainly general information, you use the information provided in consumer-firm transactions to match supply and demand. The theory of market depends on the idea that buy-sell transactions quickly and accurately provide highly reliable information about what consumers want, so that firms can accurately calibrate actions to meet demand.

You do not have to be a free market purist to see that even countries such as China and Vietnam, which renounce market principles on ideological grounds, eventually cannot compete globally unless they allow markets to operate. This is not an all-or-nothing proposition. There are "side constraints" such as taxation and the prohibition of child labor and unsafe work conditions. Most countries seek a balance between the efficiency of unconstrained markets and "side constraints" that limit the actions that can be taken in pursuit of profit.

When an action is guided by what the ethics eye reveals in a specific situation, there is lot of information in this "transaction" as well. Just as the market uses various tools, such as currency, to increase its efficiency, our tools help the ethics eye to function better. The information generated from use of the ethics eye is information about how those actually involved in situations make an *ethics* choice, just as the market reveals a *consumer* choice. This is the information upon which general ethical principles and ultimately laws and regulations should be built. Of course, there are "side constraints" here as well. For example, people who would act charitably in a specific situation may be less generous when their ethics eye is asked to operate at a distance. That is why we built such tools as *standing in the shoes* and the *global benefit approach* into the methodology for using the ethics eye.

Does the acknowledgment of the ethics eye and the tremendous amount of source information it provides mean that laws and regulations that enforce consistency should always be avoided? Does this way of looking at things drive you toward a minimalist view of the role of government—a sort of ethics libertarianism?

Our process for reaching ethical agreement, the Convergence Process, shows that it may be possible to reach ethical agreement in many of the cases in which we now use the power of policy and law without bothering to seek consensus. The ethics hierarchy goes from specific situations in which our ethics sense operates best, to principles consolidating insights derived from specific situations, to the laws and regulations required to achieve consistency and stability. Not every law has a solid ethical foundation, such as the laws outlawing euthanasia and those prohibiting certain forms of international payments (see Chapter Nine). Consideration should be given to allowing those situations to be decided by ethics and not the law. But there are also many laws intended to ensure public safety and welfare and to maintain the viability of the state. What we learn from employing the ethics eye is not to avoid laws and regulations, but to avoid imposing laws and regulations until we have done our best to reach an ethical consensus.

In the following two chapters we look at two "big issues" in ethics with a focus on using our ethics sense to build consensus.

SITUATION #10 *Easy Conscience (continued)*

Our terminal patient refuses, for religious reasons, to allow the plug (on further therapeutic treatment) to be pulled, but on the other hand requests that everything possible be done to reduce his pain. While my position on this case may strike you as harsh, I do not think you can permit administration of a level of painkillers sure to result in death, unless the patient fully understands and consents to what is happening. The patient is asking his caregivers to accept responsibility for his death, while avoiding this responsibility himself. There are many permutations and coloring facts in any situation such as this one. For example, we might ask if the patient created or will create an "advanced directive" or "living will" saying what care he does and does not want. Does the ethics eye support my position? The ethics eye is highly dependent on our ability to sympathize and empathize with those involved in a situation, and it is hard not to sympathize with the patient in this case. But our empathetic response says that were I in the patient's shoes, I would want to take responsibility for what happens to me. I could not put my family and caregivers in a situation in which they may consider themselves murderers. When I look at all of the interests involved in this case, I still think the patient has to make the choice. As with many ethical decisions guided by the ethics eye, the question comes down to who should make the decision and not whether the decision itself should go one way or another.

Chapter Nine

Ethics and Laws

"The gods visit the sins of the fathers upon the children."

—Euripedes (*Phrixius*, fragment 970)

It is often said that many of today's adults, especially so-called baby boomers, formed their ethics in the 1960s and early 1970s. When people say this, they are probably thinking of a defective ethical orientation that originated in this period with echoes continuing to this day. I suppose they are thinking of "loose" sexual mores ("free love"), a permissive attitude towards recreational drugs ("turn on, tune in, drop out"), and a rejection of authority ("off the pigs"). I was a teenager during much of this period and don't quite remember it that way, which probably means that I was an outsider. Whatever the truth about the ethics of the 1960s and early 1970s, there is no question that Watergate was one of the defining events of that period. Seeing how we responded to Watergate not only gives us insight into the issue of international bribery, it also teaches a lesson on legislating with a blind ethics eye.

Since the Watergate scandal may be outside the memory of anyone under 50, I briefly reprise the main facts. In June of 1972 there was a burglary at the offices of the Democratic National Committee, which were located in a prestigious office-residential complex in Washington, D.C., called the Watergate. The five burglars bungled the break-in and were caught. The plan to commit the burglary was traced back at least to the Oval Office, and probably to President Nixon himself. In terms of the ethical influence of Watergate, the Senate hearings on Watergate were probably the most important factor. These hearings were televised on the major networks and riveted the attention of much of the public. The hearings revealed pettiness, dishonesty, and crudeness in the White House. The hearings went on interminably, as the Senators clearly enjoyed the spotlight, and the public grew increasingly disgusted. President Nixon resigned from office to avoid being removed.

Anytime there is an opportunity to cash in on a public crisis or scandal, we do the only honorable thing—we wring our hands and hold hearings, lots of hearings, unattended hearings, televised hearings, blue-ribbon panel hearings, and so on. The Watergate scandal was milked for all it was worth. At one of these hearings it was alleged that the burglary, which cost about $50,000, may have been funded through a contribution made to the Republican National Committee by the Lockheed Corporation, a corporation that regularly fed at the public trough. This raised the possibility that U.S. tax dollars may have been used to subvert a presidential election. The spotlight was on Lockheed, and what this spotlight revealed outside of Watergate proved more interesting than what was revealed pertaining to Watergate, for the funds in question were allegedly part of a slush fund that Lockheed used to bribe officials of foreign governments—the ethical crux of the matter for us.

BRIBE OR COMMISSION?

I ask you to consider a hypothetical scenario, although I believe it to be close to the truth.

Suppose you run a company that has built a wonderful jumbo jetliner. The company built this jetliner without any orders in hand and with encouragement and funding from the U.S. government. The reasoning was that this jetliner was so much better than and unlike its predecessors that the orders would follow once the plane was demonstrated and proven practical. But the orders never materialized and you find yourself as the CEO of a company headed straight to oblivion.

And then the miraculous happens. The flag airline of Japan places a huge order for the new planes—the order you need to turn everything around.

The planes are built and ready to be delivered, but the Japanese government will not permit them in the country. No explanation is provided.

You personally take charge of the situation. You go to Japan to find out what is wrong and, hopefully, get over the hurdle. What you discover is that various members of the Japanese government, including several members of Japan's Diet, will not allow delivery unless they are paid a "commission" on each delivered aircraft. The amount of money being requested is negligible ($5,000 per official) compared to what many European government officials demand as bribes in like circumstances. (Remember, this is happening in the 1970s.) You are uncomfortable paying the "commissions" but have to think about the jobs of thousands of workers, tens of thousands of shareholders, and the many communities in which your company does business. You reason that the "commissions" are not bribes since your company has already won the business. These "commissions" are being extorted from the company. So you pay the "commissions."

I believe this scenario to be close to what actually happened in the Lockheed situation.

While these payments were probably legal under U.S. law at the time, they were embarrassing enough that many heads rolled, including those of the company's CEO and Japan's Prime Minister. There were other revelations about "commissions" paid to officials of European governments, but the Europeans took this in stride, calling for the heads of no officials.

The U.S. government had two responses. One was to launch a national investigation of government contractors called "Project Ill Wind." This investigation has never been concluded to this day. The second is that a law was passed in 1977 called the Foreign Corrupt Practices Act (FCPA). This law was intended to outlaw such "commissions" or bribes when paid by U.S.-domiciled companies. The intention was to rid governments of corruption; it was anticipated that other countries would pass similar laws outlawing bribes paid by their own companies.

I opposed this law for reasons that I shall soon explain.[11]

THE ETHICS LAW

Nothing much happened for 25 years after the FCPA was passed.[12] Foreign officials continued to solicit bribes. The only change was that these bribes were now paid by foreign companies obtaining new business at the expense of U.S. companies. There was no decrease in global corruption. The governments of some European countries even set up loosely disguised agencies to help their domestic companies pay the bribes.

One of the reasons that little happened for 25 years is that the FCPA did not imbue a particular agency of the U.S. government with the authority to enforce it. This led to a multi-decade, interagency cat fight that still has not entirely ended. In theory at least, the U.S. Department of Justice and the Securities and Exchange Commission are jointly charged with enforcing the FCPA. The cat fight was a standoff.

After little enforcement for decades, the FCPA has become an important topic for U.S. companies today. Three decades late, the European Union (EU) has moved (weakly) toward limiting bribery by EU companies. Meanwhile, in a bizarre turn of events, the U.S. Department of Justice announced that it would prosecute cases *against U.S. companies* based on complaints made by foreign governments and foreign companies. The complaints have been forthcoming, including complaints that originated in countries notorious for allowing bribery by their own domestic companies. We now have the curious situation in which the U.S. Department of Justice is prosecuting U.S. companies on behalf of their foreign competitors without demanding a reciprocal right for U.S. companies.

One problem with the FCPA is that it is very, very hard to understand. For example, the FCPA outlaws bribes but allows what it calls "grease" payments. A "grease" payment is a payment to a government official to get the official to perform duties he is otherwise obligated to perform (as opposed to a payment to obtain new business). You can imagine the legal fees that little distinction has generated. In an attempt to decode the FCPA, the U.S. Department of Justice and the Securities and Exchange Commission have jointly published a 130-page "simplifying" document titled *A Resource Guide to the U.S. Foreign Corrupt Practices Act*. We are to imagine someone trying to sell windows in China while carrying around this magnum opus. It does contain useful information. For example, if you have lunch with an M.D. or college professor in Europe, that may count as an illegal bribe, since many M.D.s and college professors are government employees in Europe, making them "foreign officials." And their official duties do not require that they lunch with you.

Instead of curing corruption, a front on which there has been slight progress, we have made Americans living overseas think twice about having lunch at McDonald's with their French professor. Or maybe that is a "grease" payment.

BRIBERY RECONSIDERED

I said that I opposed this law decades ago. Why would an "ethics guy" oppose an anti-bribery law? Let's review the situation the CEO faced in our hypothetical case. We will use our tools for sharpening the ethics eye, starting with *reading the ground rules.*

The CEO's ground rules probably included at least the following:

1. Never bribe a government official.

2. Never submit to extortion.

3. Keep promises to employees, customers, shareholders, and other interested parties.

4. Observe the laws of the United States and the other countries in which you do business.

5. Put the interests of the company and its constituencies before your personal interests.

Some of these ground rules will be broken no matter what the CEO does. If he pays the "commissions" or bribes, which he considers extortion payments, he violates at least the first and second ground rules. If he does not pay the "commissions" or bribes, he will violate the third and fifth ground rules. To the best of his knowledge, assuming that our hypothetical case is in the early 1970s, the commissions or bribes being requested were not illegal in either the United States or Japan. From the perspective of the ground rules, there is no clear direction as to whether or not to pay the "commissions" or bribes.

When we look at the CEO's choice by *finding the interests* of the affected parties, we can see that paying the "commissions" or bribes will serve many interests, specifically including the interests of those who depend on the company for a living or for the prudent use of funds invested in it. However, paying the "commissions" or bribes does not serve the interests of the citizens of the countries whose officials have solicited the payments. Payment of the "commissions" or bribes reinforces these officials in the belief that they can prosper at the expense of their citizens. Further, paying the "commissions" or bribes also may not serve the interests of the CEO, who will be held personally accountable if things go wrong. There are interests on both sides of this issue.

When you are dealing with one set of well-identified interests (those who depend on the company) and another set of interests that are comparatively remote (citizens of countries whose officials are bribed), it is a good idea to test the evaluation of interests using the *global benefit approach*. When we look at the CEO's situation in this way, in terms of *everyone* who may be affected by his actions, we find the argument most commonly used to support the FCPA. The argument is that while paying the "commissions" or bribes will benefit certain clearly identified parties, it will also reinforce a pattern of corruption that disrupts markets and encourages corrupt officials to stay in power. This, it is argued, is a negative consequence or harm to a greater number of people than those who will benefit if the bribes or "commissions" are paid.

We have already addressed this argument by noting that the CEO's actions, even if he refuses to pay the "commissions" or bribes, probably will not decrease the net amount of bribery or corruption. It will simply change the name and nationality of those paying the bribes. If the CEO pays the bribes or "commissions," he is doing no more or less than taking the place of the next person in line.

When I go through this process, I am inclined, with distinct reservations, to go along with the decision our CEO actually made: to pay the "commissions" or bribes. I would be tempted to disclose that I had made these payments once the planes were delivered and integrated into the operations of the airline buying them. But I would probably decline to do so. Why? The media will use the word "bribe," and those who hear this word will pillory both me and my company.

UNINTENDED CONSEQUENCES

What about the FCPA itself? The avowed purpose of the law was to reduce international corruption when other countries followed our lead and passed similar laws governing their domestic companies. By and large, there was no such effect for 25 years or more. Even today, no foreign country sues their own domestic companies at the behest of U.S. companies that complain. There is no way to determine how many jobs have been lost due to FCPA, but it is surely a significant number. Right now, many countries are competing for Africa's natural resources. Try as we may, we lag far behind China and European companies in this area, and the FCPA is almost certainly one reason for this.

While the FCPA was passed to prevent bribes to foreign officials, it is arguable that the payments contemplated by our CEO would be legal under the FCPA. For the FCPA allows "grease payments," payments intended to get public officials to do what they are otherwise obliged to do. I think the officials were obliged to accept delivery of the planes.

If the FCPA had been conditioned upon the enactment of parallel laws overseas, things might have worked out much differently—and better. Those who supported the FCPA failed to create the agreement necessary to its success.

Even though the motivation for the FCPA was ethical—to reduce corruption—it has served no ethical purpose to date. You are not treating ethics seriously if you react to a word like "bribery" without looking at the implications of so reacting. Some of the words we use in ethics, including "bribery," have great rhetorical power. You are not furthering the cause of ethics if you hear an ethical trigger word like "bribery" or "corruption" and act to "outlaw" it. You need to consider what will actually happen and who will be affected. Not only did the FCPA fail to achieve its stated purpose of reducing bribery globally, it also cost a lot of innocent people in the United States their jobs.

Your ethics sense will help you see what is right if you take the time to understand a situation *before* making a judgment. But when you make an ethical judgment without applying your ethics sense, and the tools designed to sharpen it, you are prone to making bad judgments. When you memorialize these judgments in laws, you make a bad decision even worse.

The FCPA was part of a storm of "ethics laws" that the generations of the 1960s and 1970s passed. Our reaction to Watergate was to punish businesses only marginally related to the break-in. Most of the sins of Watergate were committed by public officials, and not by an airplane company. The idea, born of the power politics of the 1960s and 1970s, that you can changes ethics by changing laws depends on the presumption that those with the power to change laws know what is ethical and unethical and what should and should not be permitted under the law. I know of nothing in ethics to support the idea that the power to make laws is correlated with good ethical judgment.

Chapter Ten

Ethics-Based Healthcare Reform

Healthcare is the source of many profound ethical issues. Part of the reason for this is intrinsic to healthcare and part is our own doing. Health care is intrinsically ethically complex because it deals with matters of identity, life, birth, suffering, and death. These are ethically complex topics in their own right, and they become even more so when you stir money into the mix.

This intrinsic ethical complexity is compounded many times over by the way we have chosen to pay for healthcare. We seem to have found a way to get the least amount of healthcare for the most money. It is often extremely difficult, if not outright impossible, for our ethics sense to guide our choices at the nexus of money and healthcare.

THEN AND NOW

While there are many stories of "the days when healthcare was good," I will indulge in one more such story, one I know to be true.

When my grandmother was in her mid 80s, she began to want to see our family doctor, Dr. Helling, more often. As far as her children and grandchildren could tell, some of her complaints were real and some were fanciful. Someone always had to take her on these trips to see the doctor and participate with her in Dr. Helling's debrief. She would almost always leave with either a liquid potion (which we suspected of including codeine) or a bag of brightly colored pills. In most cases, these were sugar pills. I know because I had taken them many times as a child under Dr. Helling's care. The older she got, the more time Dr. Helling allowed for her visits. If there were something seriously wrong, he would tell us. But often he said, "This should make her feel better, but let me know if she really does have something." These visits made my grandmother's life more secure and made her more comfortable with the healthcare system later when she needed to be. In case you think that this was ineffective folk medicine, both Dr. Helling and my grandmother lived to be 93.

If this scenario played out today, Dr. Helling would have purchased himself a one-way ticket to federal prison. Suppose, for example, he had billed Medicare, which did not yet exist, for the office visit. He would have to supply a diagnosic code, and "worried old lady" is not in the code book. You may think that he could have billed for psychotherapy, but he did not do psychotherapy—he was just being nice. He would have violated the Federal False Claims Act for submitting a "false" bill to a federally funded program and, since he did so knowingly, he would be subject to criminal penalties. He then gave my grandmother a prescription, which he suspiciously provided himself, for a fake medication. There goes his license. Finally, he discussed her medical condition with family members without her written consent, which is a violation of the Health Insurance Portability and Accountability Act. Dr. Helling would now be considered one of those unethical doctors fraudulently exploiting his patients and the government.

While my story may be nostalgic, it underscores the immense ethical problems in healthcare today. Dr. Helling worked for his patients. As far as anyone could tell, he had no fixed fee schedule. For example, when the local steelworkers were out on strike, he would still treat them, sometimes charging a dollar or two. If you went to see him in mink and he thought you could actually afford the mink, you paid fair market value, more or less. Why then have we made medicine practiced in the manner of Dr. Helling both a malpractice and a crime?

An Abundance of Fraud

Our federal government believes that healthcare is riddled with fraud and abuse. When President Obama ran for his first presidency, his website stated that there was enough fraud and abuse in healthcare to subsidize healthcare for every American. Each year brings more billion dollar plus healthcare fraud settlements. Even organized crime has targeted healthcare, running schemes ranging from faking Medicare numbers to running "pain clinics," which dispense vast amounts of narcotics daily. Individuals who buy health insurance may later find themselves without coverage and owing their insurance company thousands of dollars, because the insurance company has rescinded their policy retroactively. Doctors prescribe drugs based on marketing presentations and, in some cases, because the drug manufacturer pays them generously to run clinical trials. People have hips and knees implanted that are known to be badly designed and prone to failure. Patients are admitted as in-patients to hospitals where they are treated in a hallway, even though they are billed the full price of a room. Thousands of patients are owed refunds for services that both they and their insurance paid for, but the refunds are hard to come by—if anyone can even figure out what is owed to whom. Few of us can even understand the medical bills that we or our insurance are supposed to pay.

When a system is incredibly complex, understandable by few, and flush with money, it is vulnerable to corruption. When the Patient Protection and Affordable Care Act (PPACA)—commonly referred to as "healthcare reform"—passed, I asked a healthcare lawyer presenting at one of my seminars to bring a copy of PPACA along and explain its main points. It took two large boxes to hold a copy of this thousand-page-plus law, which has subsequently been modified and made even more complex.

How did we go from a system of simplicity to one of profound complexity that is riddled with fraud?

We actually designed the system almost perfectly to encourage fraud and other unethical conduct.

In Dr. Helling's day, payment for healthcare was governed mainly by market and social forces. Insurance was not yet a big part of the picture. If Dr. Helling charged too much, word would get out and either a new doctor would come to town or people would go to the next city for medical care. And Dr. Helling might not have been welcome at the next meeting of the many charitable groups to which he contributed. Health insurance reduced the role that the market and community play.

You Get What You Pay for

There are two models for healthcare payment when insurance is part of the picture. Under one model, the "indemnity" model, insurance pays for virtually all medical services, with co-pays and deductibles used to deter excessive use. This is the model for most of Medicare.[13] Under the second model, the "managed care" model, primary care doctors are paid a fixed amount for each patient, and typically get incentive pay based on their ability to avoid referrals to expensive specialists. In a variation on this model, patients can only see physicians within a defined network, and the physicians are paid an agreed upon and deeply discounted rate in order to participate in the network, thus requiring that the physician see a vast number of patients. Medicaid, which varies from state to state, mostly follows one of the managed care models.

Within the indemnity model, the more services that are provided the more money the physician makes, creating an incentive for overuse. There is ample evidence that this model incentivizes excess services.

Under the managed care model, the physician typically makes money for operating like a health club. The more people you sign up, especially healthy people, and the fewer of them that use services, the more money you make. On a variation of this model, the physician makes more money the more people he sees and the less service he provides to them.

So either way, we have a system that incentivizes healthcare providers to provide the wrong amount of care, too much or too little.

When Medicare and Medicaid came along in 1965, trillions of federal and state dollars were pumped into healthcare. This had the entirely predictable effect of dramatically increasing the cost of healthcare.

Seeing the rise in healthcare spending, the federal government intervened. A system was developed according to which reimbursement was to be tied to a system of codes. These are called ICD 9 or 10 (International Classification of Diseases) codes and CPT (Current Procedural Terminology) codes. In theory, the doctor picks the right codes, and payment follows the assigned codes.

Of course, this creates a tremendous incentive to overdiagnose patients and this is exactly what happened. There is a whole industry of consultants who teach doctors and hospitals how to "upcode" to their maximum advantage.

If you asked the leading economic minds in the world how to drive up healthcare costs, they could not do a better job than what we have done in the name of managing these costs.

In addition to all of these factors driving up the cost of healthcare, we have a litigious environment in which it is fairly easy to win malpractice lawsuits against doctors. Doctors, being human, have an error rate. But if a doctor is sued, "It was in my error rate" is not a compelling defense. Most juries know that doctors have malpractice insurance and think they can benefit the patient without harming "anyone." (Few juries are passionate about defending the interests of insurance companies.) In addition to driving up the cost of healthcare, the risk of litigation makes doctors practice medicine in a highly defensive, expensive manner in which no number of tests is too many.

Some believe that if healthcare professionals stick to their professional standards, these misplaced incentives should not significantly affect the practice of medicine. This is a bet on ground rules trumping interests. Unfortunately, this bet is misplaced. The thing about incentive schemes is that they work. In the case of healthcare, we have incentivized two styles of healthcare, neither of which puts the patient first.

Even though no one admits that we have promulgated deformed incentive schemes, healthcare reform—PPACA—includes yet another incentive scheme meant to remedy the harm caused by earlier incentive schemes. Under PPACA, healthcare providers earn extra money if they simultaneously reduce costs and improve quality. While healthcare reform is basically a variation on managed care, the idea is to short circuit the temptation to underserve patients by adding incentives for quality into the mix. But this approach is dead on arrival. Rather than promoting quality as envisioned by patients, the government will set its own standards, most of which remain speculative. Once these standards become apparent, we will see that we have created an incredibly sharp, and likely effective, incentive for committing fraud by misapplying the quality measures. Additionally, we have incentivized providers to avoid risky populations. Consider this provider decision: I can do a procedure with a 30% chance of success on a patient who will otherwise die. A 30% chance is better than no chance. However, I will be taking money out of my own pocket by doing so, since failure, the more likely outcome, counts against my quality measures.

THE ETHICS APPROACH

It is, of course, one thing to point out what is wrong with healthcare and quite another to do something about it. If we put what is wrong with healthcare in the simplest terms, it is that most incentive schemes don't work when the buyer of a service is not the payer for the service. And this is exactly what happens when insurance or the government, acting as an insurer, pays for healthcare. But short of traveling backward in time, is there an approach that will better align the interests in healthcare with what is best for patients?

Let's see if what we have learned in sharpening our ethics sense can help us find a better path.

Our strategy in sharpening our ethics sense has been to work from the specific toward the general. Using observations of the ethics eye in specific situations, we can move toward general principles. By this standard, what we have done wrong in healthcare is that we have tried to direct care from the top down through policies and incentives not based on ethically sound, specific healthcare decisions. What we are seeing in healthcare is a not uncommon side effect of centralized planning. We are trying to control supply and demand instead of letting individual decisions do so. If we want to fix what is wrong, we should try paying for healthcare based on what is right in the specific situations in which healthcare decisions are made. In other words, we need to see what happens when the patient, the payer, and the provider are in a close communication relationship.

My employers or I have paid healthcare premiums for me every month since I was 20 years old. For all practical purposes, I made no use of my health insurance for the first 25 years of my career. Suppose now that a part of my premium had been retained based on how much I used my health insurance. If my premiums for a given year totaled $6,000, and I only used $1,000 in benefits, half of the $5,000 difference would be put into an account for my benefit. That benefit could be used to pay for my health insurance in later years, when health insurance is more costly, or simply treated as an annuity toward my retirement. If I used more healthcare in a year than I paid in premiums, half the amount exceeding the premium would be withdrawn from my account. Even if I had a catastrophic illness, the maximum I would owe is my premium. (That is why I am only getting half of my unused premium back. I am buying insurance against a catastrophic event.) True, a catastrophic illness might liquidate my annuity account but that is no different than my current situation. However, I now have a powerful financial incentive to avoid catastrophic events.

Let's test this approach against some specific situations.

Suppose that I develop a backache. I can either go to the doctor or wait for a few days and see if it goes away. I wait but it doesn't go away, so I go to the doctor. The doctor tells me that I can either have costly back surgery with a good chance of success or start a fitness regime that might make the surgery unnecessary. My basic interest is in getting well, but I also want to preserve my healthcare account. My interest in my own well-being (getting well without the risks of surgery) and my interest in my healthcare annuity (not blowing it on potentially unnecessary surgery) both point toward trying the fitness regime before considering the surgery.

How does the ethics-based model look from the perspective of a primary care provider? On this model, a doctor wins by attracting patients who use her or his services. If the doctor is too expensive or too quick with the scalpel, she or he will have a problem attracting patients. Patients will be guarding their own funds and not just those of an insurer. The doctor's incentive is to let patients participate in decision making concerning their own care by being mindful of their economic interests as well as their physical interests.

Let's test this model against an end-of-life decision.

Suppose that I am 75 years old and have been paying health insurance premiums (or having them paid on my behalf) for 50 years. I have a grave illness and on the most optimistic estimates, I have two months to live. With a highly costly treatment regime, I might add 30 days to my life. But the cost of the treatment will exhaust the very large balance in my healthcare annuity and deprive my heirs of all benefit from the annuity. If I go ahead with the treatment, much of its cost will be paid for with my own money. If I decide against the treatment—and I have a powerful incentive to so decide—I preserve part of my estate for my heirs. Again, I think we come up with sensible answers.

I do not suggest that this ethics-based approach to healthcare would be easy to implement. Our dysfunctional healthcare system is so entrenched that it would be hard for even a perfect alternative to be implemented. On the other hand, we could gradually start the ethics-based model for individuals newly entering the work force and eventually move away from systems that incentivize too much or too little healthcare.

The important point is that by recognizing our ethics sense and the circumstances in which it is most reliable, we can at least think of a new approach to a seemingly intractable problem. Using what we know about the ethics eye, we can see that current healthcare approaches don't work, because they depend on decisions being made in circumstances in which our ethics sense is less likely to be effective. And we can at least find a direction in which our ground rules regarding healthcare, our interests, and our ethical decision making are aligned. We now have a chance to take actions to make an ethical difference, if only gradually.

This often happens when you bring the ethics sense into complex issues of social policy. You find new approaches that are not otherwise evident and you avoid approaches that, by their very structure, minimize, or eliminate the operation of the ethics sense.

Chapter Eleven

Move Forward with Confidence

Heart of Africa

While this case goes back many years, to a time before apartheid was abandoned in South Africa, it is one of the most challenging of my career. One important lesson I learned from this case, and use in my ethics work, is that the job of the CEO of a public company is much more complex than the standards by which CEOs are judged.

A U.K.-based multinational company was struggling with the issue of whether or not to continue doing business in South Africa. The CEO of the company was firmly opposed to discrimination in general and to apartheid in particular. He found apartheid disgusting. The problem was that the company had been operating in South Africa for more than 50 years. Rather than go along with apartheid, the company had sidestepped it. It paid its black workers and white workers comparable wages and provided a full range of educational and health benefits to its black employees. Many of the black graduates of the company's schools had gone on to achieve college educations at some of Europe's finest universities. Some South African employees had more than 40 years' tenure with the company. Many of the company's educated black employees would be unable to find comparable work outside the company.

The CEO felt that the company did not have to be ashamed of its actions. On the other hand, it was going along with a separate but equal approach and also producing revenue for a government that supported apartheid. While the company was a large employer in South Africa, it did not have the influence to move the government off its support of apartheid. There was also no question in the CEO's mind that the boycott of South Africa by European businesses was having an effect. The effect was not so much on supplies or markets for South Africa, which still had a number of client states. But by bringing the plight of South African blacks to the center of Europe's politics, the South African government was feeling increasingly isolated. If the company did not support the boycott, it was sure to be the object of protests and union actions at home, and its products might end up being boycotted by some domestic consumers.

The CEO was so troubled by this decision that he dispatched emissaries to visit with leaders of the country's anti-apartheid groups to seek their input on the company's decision.

If the CEO used our ethics tools to reach a conclusion, which way would he go? You may be surprised to read the actual outcome at the end of the chapter.

Suppose you know the right thing to do, but just don't do it? The ancient Greeks called this phenomenon "ακρασια (*akrasia*)." We sometimes explain this by saying things like "He knew what he should do but lacked the courage" or "She knew what was right but wanted someone else to take the lead" or even "He knew what was right, but that made little difference to a person of his character." When I work as an ethics advisor, I find these outcomes unacceptable. I am not seeking knowledge that stops short of action because of an excuse. That is called wasting your time.

Many things can keep us from doing what is right, even when we know what the right thing to do is. One of the most common causes is that we simply do not have confidence in our innate ethics sense. We have already seen some of the reasons for this, which include the idea that someone with special knowledge, whether scientific, religious, or spiritual, is arbiter of right and wrong. Another reason is that we have done what we thought was right in the past but later regretted it. Regret normally includes the judgment that our past action was not the right thing to do. And sometimes we do not do what is right because we are waiting for someone else to do it.

THE BYSTANDER EFFECT

One of the most notable examples of knowing what is right but not doing it is the Kitty Genovese case from 1964. Kitty Genovese was a young woman who was walking from her car to the entrance of her apartment complex about 100 feet away. She was attacked by a robber and stabbed as she ran from him. She crawled to the entrance of her building screaming for help, but no one helped her although several residents admitted to seeing her or hearing her screams. The robber returned, robbed her of $49, raped her, and stabbed her a second time clearly within sight and hearing of the building. She died. While the occupants of the building were at least somewhat aware of her plight, none intervened to help her. As far as can be determined, each observer knew he or she should intervene but felt that confronting the robber could be left to someone else. This is sometimes called the bystander effect.

The truth is that if you have followed a sound process for ensuring that your ethics sense sees the right thing, you should have confidence in doing what you see as right. What the proper use of the ethics eye reveals is the foundation, the body of data, on which all theories, opinions, and principles about right and wrong are built. If a brilliant theory tells you that you will see a polka dot sky tomorrow morning, and you wake up to a blue sky, the theory wasn't so brilliant after all. Your senses trump the theory no matter how brilliant the theory. None of our senses are 100% reliable. In a particular case, we might think we see something when we really don't. Perhaps we have taken a hallucinogenic drug, have poor vision, or are very suggestible. Still, the way we judge whether someone's senses are working is by using our own senses working under better conditions.

So it is with the ethics sense. We may be wrong in particular cases, but the way we know that we were wrong in those cases is that our ethics sense tells us that we were wrong once we know more or have a better perspective on the case.

The only difference between the ethics sense and our other senses is that we have been talked out of recognizing this sense for many years—or told to distrust it by various "authorities." We have learned several ways to improve the functioning of the ethics sense, and there are certain to be many more. But that does not mean that we should lack confidence in using it until we have reduced the margin of error to zero.

A friend asked me how I can have so much confidence in the ethics sense when people who otherwise appeared normal authored the atrocities committed by the Nazis during World War II. My answer is that if the individuals who committed these atrocities had engaged their powers of sympathy and empathy with respect to the victims of their crimes, their ethics sense would have told them that what they were doing was wrong. Instead, these individuals consciously decided not to extend their sympathy, empathy, and ethics sense to a class of individuals. These atrocities are testimony to the extent which the grip of ideology can corrupt the ethics sense. And that is why our process for using the ethics sense is designed to short circuit ideologies that stunt the thoughts and emotions that power the ethics sense.

USE YOUR SENSE

I do not ask you to agree with me that we have found *the* process for ensuring the operation of the ethics sense. We have denied the validity of our ethics sense for so long that we are only starting to sharpen our ethical vision. It took hundreds of years for our five senses to build a scientific edifice in which we can have confidence. Imagine how hard this would have been if someone had convinced us that vision cannot be relied upon in learning how the world works. Acting according to our ethics sense, and learning from those actions, is the path for those who want to make an ethical difference.

I will be excited as readers improve on what they find of value in *Make an Ethical Difference*. If we see that ethical knowledge starts with the use of our innate ethics sense in specific situations, we can fully expect to change our views as we continue to learn more by using this sense. But there will be no feedback and no potential for learning from our ethical mistakes if we lack the confidence to act on what our ethics sense tells us is the right thing to do.

SITUATION #11 *Heart of Africa (continued)*

Our CEO visited the company's South African employees, who numbered in the thousands, and the company town in which many of them lived. He wanted to *stand in their shoes*. The company's emissaries to the anti-apartheid groups came back with surprising news. The response was that they did

162

not want to see more of their constituents thrust into poverty. They suggested that the company remain in South Africa, publicly explain its reasons for staying despite its objections to apartheid, and work with the anti-apartheid groups to end apartheid. The CEO was deeply moved by the appeals of the company's South African employees, and contrary to many of his closest peers, the company stayed in South Africa to see the end of apartheid. Many of his company's South African employees and their children have played a key role in the first post-apartheid governments. Was it the right decision? There is no question that the boycott and threatened boycotts of South Africa by European and U.S. companies played a role in ending apartheid. The CEO of this company not only stayed in South Africa, but took many actions to ensure the end of apartheid. Although the company won no corporate responsibility awards, I believe that such awards would not be needed if other CEOs took the same care to use their ethics sense as this CEO did.

Resources for Action

This section summarizes and focuses the tools we have developed for seeing and doing the right thing. When you face an ethical situation, you want practical tools readily at hand—not buried in a book. This section gives you a set of tools in a clear and usable form.

The tools fall into two categories. The first category consists of tools to sharpen your own ethics sense. The second category consists of tools to achieve ethical agreement with others. Tools of these two kinds are not independent of one another. The process of seeking ethical agreement with others often sharpens your own ethics sense. On the other hand, sharpening your own ethics sense may help you figure out how to achieve ethical agreement with others.

The Five Tools

We start by reviewing the tools for sharpening our own ethics sense.

TOOL #1 *Read the Ground Rules*

When a situation presents an ethical issue, *look beyond the individuals and their actions and uncover the ground rules* that help explain their actions. Remember that ground rules are rules that will only be breached *under extreme duress.*

If a situation involves groups or organizations as well as individuals, do the same thing for each group or organization. Read their ground rules.

Write out the ground rules of the affected parties as specifically as possible. Rather than working with generalizations that don't tell you much in the situation, drill down to the ground rules actually at issue. If the ground rules you have written down are not helping you make sense of the situation, get more specific.

Remember that the organization or organizations involved in the situation have ground rules, too.

Reading the ground rules not only helps you understand why certain things happen and certain things don't happen, you can also understand *what you have to change—* the ground rules—to be a successful ethical change agent.

TOOL #2   *Reason Backward to Find the Interests*

When you confront an ethical issue or problem, you need to know what interests are at stake. This includes not only the interests of individuals, but also the interests of groups and organizations. Unstated or hidden interests are often the key to resolving ethical issues.

The best way to *find the interests* is to reason backward from an outcome desired by someone to the interest or interests served by that outcome. Ask of each possible outcome, "What interests will that outcome serve and for whom?"

Do not be quick to settle on a single or obvious interest. Most outcomes can serve many interests, and there is a tendency to hide a personal interest behind a public interest.

Reasoning backward from outcomes to interests gives you a good picture of the interests in a situation. But there are also cases in which you will find that there is still something missing. There are two reasons for not finding relevant interests. There may be hidden *parties* to a situation. Or there may be outcomes that have not yet been considered. *Always supplement reasoning backward by asking, "Who else might be affected?" and "Are there outcomes that haven't been considered?"*

When thinking about an ethical problem or issue, it is a good idea to list the outcomes, both declared and undeclared, under consideration. Once you have listed the outcomes, correlate each one with the interests served by it. Describe the outcomes and related interests as specifically as possible.

When you know only some of the interests, your ethics sense tries to find a solution based only on those interests. Knowing all of the interests means you can view the facts of the situation with less risk of bias and in full knowledge of who may be affected and how.

Combine *finding the interests* with *reading the ground rules*. When associating interests with outcomes, you can also associate ground rules with each outcome. Each outcome may not only advance or fail to advance certain interests; it may also be either consistent or inconsistent with the ground rules of the parties to the situation.

Seek outcomes that advance many interests without violating the ground rules. Everyone wins and not at the expense of anyone's ethics. These are "win right" outcomes. The parties to the situation "win" in the sense that their interests are advanced. The outcome is "right" in that it does not sacrifice ground rules to advance certain interests.

TOOL #3   *Face the Facts*

In order for your ethics sense to function properly in a given situation, you should have a good grasp of the facts. Once we have looked at the ground rules and interests, bring fact-finding into the picture. When you are looking for the right action in a situation, you have to see facts in the context of the ground rules and interests of the parties to the situation.

The first step in *facing the facts* is to look for the facts that all parties, irrespective of their ground rules and interests, agree upon. The next step is to identify the contested facts. These are the facts that one party asserts as fundamental to the matter, without the agreement of other parties to the situation. Finally, you look at any facts that are introduced by one party or another but are neither agreed upon nor contested. Now that you have the universe of facts, narrow them down to a manageable body of information.

Ask of each contested fact, "If I accepted this as true, would I change my mind about the right thing to do?" If the answer is no, you don't have to worry about that one. If the answer is yes, evaluating that contested fact may be important to what your ethics sense tells you. If this process does not bring you to a clear picture of the facts relevant to the situation, follow the same process with the facts in the third category, those that are neither agreed upon nor contested.

You have done a good job of *facing the facts* if adding more facts to the picture no longer changes what your ethics sense tells you.

Facing the facts is not really a distinct part of the process of finding the right action so much as it is interwoven with all parts of the process. As you look at the ground rules and interests in a situation, you will find that you constantly have to reevaluate the facts. As you consider additional facts, the acid test is always the same: If this were true, would it change my judgment as to what is right in the situation?

TOOL #4   *Stand in the Shoes*

When you approach a situation that poses an ethical issue, identify the individuals and groups potentially affected by what happens. This task combines naturally with *finding the interests,* since what you are doing now is giving an identity to those who have the interests.

Now that you know who is affected, reduce the distance between you and them. *Identify the affected individuals and groups that differ from you the most and meet the individuals or members of the group.*

List the affected individuals and groups most distant from you and write down their interests and ground rules, particularly ground rules that differ from your own. You will know that you have completed the task of reducing your distance from them if you are able to verify or reject each interest and ground rule. Of course, you will add interests and modify ground rules throughout the process. You are removing obstacles to the functioning of the ethics eye by bringing its objects closer.

TOOL #5   *The Global Benefit Approach*

Use the *global benefit approach* to rate the possible outcomes of your actions in terms their likely consequences. To use the *global benefit approach, ask which course of action produces the greatest balance of benefit over harm for all concerned.* The *global benefit approach* usually doesn't solve ethical problems, but it raises questions that can help solve these problems.

170

When using the *global benefit approach*, you first ask *who counts*—who the affected parties are. If you have already used *find the interests* and *stand in the shoes,* you have a good understanding of who counts. You also have to ask what is to be considered—*what counts* as a benefit or harm in considering possible outcomes.

While we want to produce as much benefit as possible, we also have to *read the ground rules* that apply to the situation. An action that produces a lot of benefit while violating important ground rules is probably not the right action. An action that produces great benefit without violating the ground rules is, however, a good candidate for being the right action.

THE CONVERGENCE PROCESS

Most things that you want to accomplish in ethics, or most other fields, require the participation of more than one individual or group. While you can use our tools for sharpening the ethics sense to find what *you* believe is the right action, you will often fail in your pursuit of that action if others do not agree with and support you.

Agreement in ethics exists when what your ethics eye shows to be the right action and what the ethic eyes of others see as the right action are the same. Our process for achieving ethical agreement, the Convergence Process, is designed to increase the alignment of the ethics eyes of those directly involved in a situation requiring action. It is a systematic way of using our tools for sharpening the ethics eye to achieve agreement in actual situations.

While the Convergence Process is a step-wise process, what you find in one step may lead you to reconsider earlier steps. For example, as your knowledge of the ground rules and interests grows, you may have to go back to earlier steps in the process to ensure that you uncovered all of the relevant facts.

Commitment to the Convergence Process involves a willingness to change your own views based on what the process shows. In other words, achieving ethical agreement is as likely to involve your beliefs as it is to involve the beliefs of others.

The Convergence Process is a methodology for creating agreement among the individuals involved in an ethical situation. While one individual can pursue this process, the likelihood of reaching ethical agreement increases as more of the parties to an ethical situation participate in the Convergence Process.

Step #1

Face the facts. Bring any facts on which the parties disagree to the surface and attempt to resolve these factual disagreements. If you have trouble agreeing on the facts, try to reach agreement on a *method* for settling the facts and apply this method. And remember that you may have to revisit the facts once you have considered the ground rules, interests, and perspectives of those affected.

Step #2

In order to see if an ethical disagreement is about ground rules, identify the ground rules of the parties to the disagreement. *Read the ground rules* common to all parties as well as those that may be the source of the disagreement. When the parties to the disagreement see the ground rules on which they agree, this may allow them to reach agreement. When the parties to the disagreement see the ground rules on which they disagree, there may be room for change on one or all sides of the disagreement.

Step #3

If the facts and ground rules don't resolve an ethical disagreement, try *finding the interests* involved in the situation. In addition to *finding the interests* of the parties to the disagreement, find the interests of the others who may be affected by the decision. To ensure coverage of interests, go beyond *finding the interests* to considering them collectively. Use the *global benefit approach* to see if there is agreement over what course of action will produce the greatest balance of benefit over harm.

Step #4

If you are unable to reach agreement based on facts, ground rules, and interests, make your focus increasingly specific. *Stand in the shoes* of others who may be critically affected by the decision. To the extent possible, make these potentially affected parties participants in your deliberations.

SITUATIONS

The following situations were discussed in the book and are summarized here so that you can use them as exercises for yourself, co-workers, or students. You may want to simplify the situations if you are using them for co-workers or students. You may also want to add facts to make the situations lean in one direction or another. Be careful not to add so many facts that the situation no longer presents a challenge. A set of solutions to these situations follows the list of situations.

SITUATION #1 *Less Is More*

Ever since the upstart Greek yogurt companies, Chobani and Fage came along, the big dogs in the yogurt industry have been hurting. For years, profits soared as they sold smaller and smaller containers of yogurt at ever higher prices. As soon as one company reduced the size of its yogurt containers, the other companies followed suit. As a bonus, they could claim to have reduced the number of calories per unit of their product, which was accomplished by making the portions smaller.

Today, one of the old-line yogurt companies is considering challenging the upstarts by introducing its own Greek yogurt at a lower price and with fewer calories. The trick is to fool consumers into thinking that its product is less expensive and less fattening simply by giving them less product per container. It worked before, so why not again? But someone in the room asks, "Is it right to compete by fooling our customers?" To which another person answers, "We never tricked anyone. We simply helped our customers to do something they should do in any case, which is to control portion size."

What advice would you give to the old-line yogurt company?

SITUATION #2   *This Land Is Your Land*

You are consulting to a company in the "raw land" business. Land is considered "raw" if it is either not currently in use or is used only for farming and has no roads or utilities. Buying such land is highly speculative because developing the land for residential or commercial use depends on approvals at many levels of government, not to mention someone willing to pay for the roads and other infrastructure. The client has a buyer for a large chunk of raw land, a huge public company whose bonds are rated AAA. When it came to the negotiations, the public company offered a reasonable price, but offered to double the price if the client would accept its AAA rated bonds instead of cash. When the public company's chief financial officer computed the value of the AAA rated bonds on offer to the client, he made a huge error in the client's favor. The only condition the public company put on its offer was that the client decide then and there. The client asked, "Should I take cash now or go for the much higher valued bonds?"

How would you advise the client in this situation?

SITUATION #3   *Outside Looking In*

One of the world's largest financial services companies faces an ethical issue. The issue is in the executive suite, and to some extent in the bedrooms of those in the executive suite. The male CEO of the company had put a lot of trust in a younger employee with whom he was having an affair. Unfortunately, the younger employee abused this trust in a way that might soon become public. Or so the board of directors feared. The board brought in "outsiders" to "gain perspective" and "contain" the problem. While the board knew that it would have to make changes in the executive team, it also knew that the story would be a juicy one in the media. The board asked, "What will our employees think once they see what their leaders have been up to?"

Your job, as one of the "outsiders," is to keep the rot from spreading from the top throughout the organization, thereby creating even more ethical problems. When the employees of an organization learn that the CEO made huge business blunders on the advice of his lover, they often conclude that the whole organization is corrupt and lower their own expectations of ethical conduct.

What would you advise the company to do?

SITUATION #4 *School's Out*

Periodically, there is an outcry over children being sexually abused in private schools. An association of one state's private schools hired an ethics advisor to help them address allegations of abuse in schools owned by its members. They were hoping that a code of conduct or a set of public ethical standards might help them offset the bad publicity.

Most abuse allegations involved private schools. One possibility was that molesters targeted these schools as places of employment because their hiring standards are more lax than those of public schools. In fact, most of the private schools did extensive background checks on employees while the public schools often didn't bother. So what was happening?

A team of people interviewed a random sample of parents with young children in school, irrespective of whether the kids went to private or public schools. The results were surprising.

The study found that at least as many parents of kids in public schools suspected abuse as did parents of kids in private schools. If the parents of a child in a private school blow the whistle on an alleged molester, they can simply put their child in a different school. But many parents of kids in public schools were reluctant to raise suspicions about a teacher because their child would probably remain in the school, possibly under the control of the alleged molester.

What approach would you recommend to the private school association?

SITUATION #5   *Borderline Ethics*

You are advising a public hospital located close to the U.S.-Mexico border. Hospitals that serve large numbers of indigent patients sometimes employ a strategy of having medical "residents" deliver services under the supervision of experienced physicians, as opposed to having experienced physicians do most of the work. Generally, there is no problem with having services delivered by residents, provided that they are properly supervised. However, the required supervision is expensive so there is a temptation to scrimp on it. This hospital had been caught doing just that and was, thus, guilty of improperly taking funds from Medicare and Medicaid. Medicare and Medicaid will pay for services delivered by a resident only if there is documented supervision.

You are invited to join the hospital's leadership and its attorneys at the offices of the U.S. Department of Justice. The amount of restitution to be paid to the U.S. government (Medicare and Medicaid) and to others (various states and private insurers) is to be determined at the meeting of all parties. Your job is to present the hospital's new ethics program and explain why it will prevent future abuses. The hospital's lawyers are arguing for a small fine based on technical legal issues. The attorneys for the government are becoming furious. Despite being guilty in the particulars at issue, it is a good hospital that has helped thousands who otherwise would have received no care.

What actions would you take in your role as an ethics advisor?

SITUATION #6   *Kneecapped*

Before I became a full time ethics advisor, I worked as an academic. One day I got a call from a Dr. Cullen (name changed) wanting to meet with me about an ethical issue. Dr. Cullen was the new head of the university's student health service.

Over the weekend, a member of the school's football team had visited the student health center, not wanting to go to the team doctor. He had a sore knee. Dr. Cullen was the only physician on duty and examined the young

178

man's knee. What he found was startling. Someone had performed *non-arthroscopic* surgery on the student's knee. The surgery was sloppy and would have to be redone with medium prospects of success. This young athlete was the first member of his family to attend college and he was expected to turn pro as soon as he completed school.

When Dr. Cullen reported this to the team doctor, the team doctor told Dr. Cullen that he was an inexperienced general practitioner and was mistaken. When Dr. Cullen reported the situation to the athletic director, he was told to take a hike.

On the face of it, Dr. Cullen was simply trying to help a member of one of the school's teams. Dr. Cullen was young and bright so I thought that maybe his know-it-all manner explained his cold reception and decided to do some research.

I learned that the athletic director had a football team booster group composed of local doctors, who paid $20,000 a year each to belong to this group. There was no qualification for joining this group except that one was a physician willing to fork out $20,000. In return for their $20,000, the boosters got decent seats, a chance to meet the players, and one more thing—they got most of the medical referrals from the athletics department. The incompetent doctor who operated on the young athlete's knee was a member of this group.

I told Dr. Cullen that I saw two options. The first was to bring the press into the picture. This would certainly ruin

MAKE AN ETHICAL DIFFERENCE

his career at the university, and probably elsewhere. On the other hand, the story could easily be confirmed and it would be front-page news in the local press, and, probably nationally. The university would not be able to hide from the situation.

Another option was to go straight to the president of the university. The president, who was relatively new to his position, could take the high ground by addressing the problem forthrightly. The problem was that the athletic director had been the new president's first significant appointment.

Dr. Cullen told me that he had written to the president and showed me the letter, which was argumentative and disrespectful. Dr. Cullen was angry and it showed. I feared that the president had reacted more to the tone of the letter than to its contents. As a newly appointed professor, I was hardly a power player at the university. If we were going to have a chance, we needed a good strategy.

What strategy would you recommend?

SITUATION #7 *Judge for Yourself*

In a seminar for a group of state judges, one of the judges asked the following question: "What you would you do if you were the judge and the prosecution brought someone before the court who was clearly guilty of the charges against him—and any number of other serious crimes, mostly against the elderly?" The problem is that the prosecution made a technical error by not showing the defense certain key documents. This probably happened because the case was so open-and-shut against the defendant that someone got sloppy. In a practical sense, there is no question about the guilt of the defendant. The defense does not know about the missing documents and need never know about them. The truth is that the judge should throw the case out on a procedural error. The problem is that this will put the culprit back on the street for an indefinite period of time, unquestionably hurting more people.

Should the judge overlook the procedural error in the interests of public safety?

SITUATION #8 *Dead River*

An ethically complex environmental issue occurred in the 1980s with respect to the Pigeon River, a river that flows through North Carolina and Tennessee. Several industrial companies, including several paper plants, had dumped their waste into the river over the years. The river remained viable and was widely used by sportsmen until dioxin was discovered in the river and a related reservoir. Dioxin tends to settle at the bottom of waterways, with the consequence that cleaning it up may have the effect of stirring it up. When the dioxin was discovered in the Pigeon River, some environmentalists began calling it "The Dead Pigeon River." Many of the companies that had dumped dioxin into the river were no longer in business, and it was unlikely that any current employee of the remaining companies was employed by the companies when the waste was dumped.

To environmentalists and some residents, it seemed obvious that the remaining companies were liable for the pollution.

Many of the employees of the companies along the Pigeon River felt that the companies could not be held responsible for actions not known to be harmful and taken long before their association with the companies. It would be like arresting a child because his parent held up a store. This argument has its limits because companies are corporate persons within the law and their lifetime is unlimited. Legally, the "corporate person" who polluted the river years ago is the same "corporate person" who employs people today.

How do you think this situation should be resolved?

SITUATION #9 *Private Interests*

A publicly traded technology company developed software for business applications and had a history of consistent earnings. The model for selling the company's software was that the software would be provided to value-added resellers who would then sell the software to customers along with a service and support package. A unit of the software package was considered sold when the reseller sold the unit to a customer. The reseller had the right to return units if they had not sold before an updated edition appeared.

The problem was that one iteration of the product was a dud and units were coming back in large volume. There was a new version that corrected the problems and it was being shipped to the resellers. However, it would be months before there were new sales. There was a risk that the company would lose its credit line and be forced into bankruptcy during the interim.

The Chief Financial Officer of the company advised the CEO that a slight change in accounting practices, still within generally accepted accounting principles, could save the day. The idea was to count units as sold when they were delivered to the reseller rather than when the reseller sold the units to a final customer. If sales were slow, as in the current circumstance, they could put a lot of product in the sales channels that would count as sold. Since resellers still had the right to return products, sales would be adjusted by the historical return rate, which, until recently, was quite low. This strategy would yield good sales numbers while the new generation of products brought sales back up to speed. The company would show consistent sales, its credit line would be intact, and, before anyone could object, the company would be back in good shape.

The CEO was intrigued by this idea since the company's external auditors signed off on the change in accounting practices. All of this could be included in a Securities and Exchange Commission filing that was unlikely to attract attention. And even if there were objections, they would take time. The company would be back on its feet by then and could adjust past earnings accordingly.

If the CEO in this situation does what is best for the company's employees, he will change accounting practices with as little notice as possible. There is also a self-interested reason for the CEO to take this approach. Most CEOs are paid in stock in large part. The CEO can hedge his personal bets by gradually selling some of his stock while the new version of the software enters the market. Of course, trades made under these conditions would be both ethically and legally suspect.

Why was ethics advice sought in this case and what is the right advice?

SITUATION #10 *Easy Conscience*

A terminal patient is in great pain but, with the concurrence of his family, refuses, for religious reasons, to allow the plug (on further therapeutic treatment) to be pulled. However, the patient requests that everything be done to reduce the pain to the maximum possible extent. The patient's physicians explain that the pain can be reduced and almost eliminated, but at the expense of the patient's consciousness and, imminently, his life. The patient and the patient's family find this consequence acceptable. The physicians, however, wonder if they are participating in an assisted suicide.

What advice would you give to the physician in charge and the family members?

SITUATION #11 *Heart of Africa*

This case occurred while apartheid was still in effect in South Africa. A U.K.-based multinational company was struggling with the issue of whether to continue doing business in South Africa. The CEO of the company found apartheid disgusting. The problem was that the company had been operating in South Africa for more than 50 years.

Rather than go along with apartheid, the company had sidestepped it. It paid its black workers and white workers comparable wages and provided a full range of educational and health benefits to its black employees. Many of the black graduates of the company's schools had gone on to achieve college educations at some of Europe's finest universities. Some employees had more than 40 years tenure with the company. Many of the company's educated and skilled black employees would be unable to find comparable work outside the company.

The CEO felt that the company did not have to be ashamed of its actions. On the other hand, it was going along with a separate but equal approach and also producing revenue for a government that supported apartheid. While the company was a large employer in South Africa, it did not have the influence to move the government off its support of apartheid. There was also no question in the CEO's mind that the boycott of South Africa by European businesses was having an effect. By bringing the plight of South African blacks to the center of Europe's politics, the South African government was feeling increasingly isolated. If the company did not support the boycott, it was sure to be the object of protests and union actions at home, and its products might end up being boycotted by some consumers.

The CEO was so troubled by this decision that he dispatched emissaries to the country's anti-apartheid groups to seek their input on the company's decision.

What advice would you give the CEO?

Solutions

While I have tried to depersonalize the solutions to some extent, in the end they represent the way I approached these situations. The solutions offered here are not *the* solutions. In most real-life ethical situations, there are many correct approaches. So feel free to use the situations while supplying your own solutions.

SOLUTION #1 *Less Is More*

My advice to the yogurt company:

You got into this predicament by using trickery to increase profits—and it worked for quite a while. However, you also made yourself vulnerable to the upstart Greek yogurt companies, and now you are paying the price. Even if you push the upstarts back with more trickery, there is no guarantee that you will succeed. Now that you have upstart competitors, they may reveal your strategy for what it is. My advice would be to at least match the quality and portions of the upstarts while working hard to out-market them. Yours is still the familiar brand and you have enormous advantages in commanding shelf space. This is the ethical way to compete, and it will also ensure that any customers you regain will stay loyal.

SOLUTION #2 *This Land Is Your Land*

I advised the client to take cash. I asked myself, "If the public corporation's finances justified the AAA rating of its bonds, why would it offer the client so much more in terms of bonds?" Another ethics warning sign was that the public corporation was putting extreme pressure on the client to decide on the spot. They didn't want the client to think the situation over and take a closer look at the public company's finances.

SOLUTION #3 *Outside Looking In*

This organization was an honest company, so the task was to keep the ground rules from slipping as a result of the soon-to-be-disclosed scandal. It was important not to compound the internal damage to the company by trying to convince the employees that what they would inevitably learn was not true. So the problem was communicating with the employees in a manner that neither hid the truth nor demoralized the company.

The board needed to clean house in the executive suite in as short a time as feasible without leaving the company rudderless. Almost everyone in the executive suite had some inkling of what was going on. In this way, if the issue did become public, the company would already have taken action. Employees would see that the improper conduct was handled decisively and that the board would be viewed as taking strong action to protect the reputation of the company.

SOLUTION #4 *School's Out*

The public school parents who were afraid to speak up formed an important interest group. Realizing that the problem affected a larger set of interests than initially considered enabled the private school association to take a much stronger stand—against abuse in *any* school. The association was able to pass a statewide requirement for strict background checks for anyone interacting with children in any kind of school. And they were able to educate parents on how to detect the signs of abuse, report concerns, and take prompt, effective action. The actions that the state association took are today's national standard for protecting children from abuse in school.

SOLUTION #5 *Borderline Ethics*

I asked myself what interests the parties brought to the negotiation. For the government attorneys, the more money they derived from the case, the better their performance would be viewed by their supervisors. The hospital's lawyers got paid no matter what happened, but seemed genuinely committed to the hospital's cause. And I thought about the insanely underserved patients of the hospital, who seemed likely to be even more underserved in the near future.

I broke into ongoing arguments among the attorneys. I decided that it was time to get past the technicalities and focus on the interests. I asked the hospital's new CEO to outline the hospital's financials for the group. The CEO apologized for the past practices and then provided a picture of the hospital's bleak financial situation showing that 45% of the care it provided was completely uncompensated. One of the lead attorneys for the Department of Justice was herself of Mexican heritage—and it was as if a light went on. If this hospital went down, a lot of people with backgrounds at least somewhat similar to her own would pay for it. She proposed a settlement far more reasonable than the hospital considered possible—one that allowed it to continue its charitable mission.

SOLUTION #6 *Kneecapped*

I decided to try another letter to the president, this time with a polite and respectful tone. I stated in my letter to him that as a new faculty member, I wanted nothing more than to see my school do the right thing.

This strategy worked well enough for me to get a half-hour appointment with the president. Instead of showing up alone, I brought Dr. Cullen, the student athlete, and the athlete's parents along. The president was furious at me but met with everyone, as he had little choice. You could almost see the light go on when he was trying to explain things to the parents. Sympathy and empathy kicked in and jarred him out of his institutional role. In the space of that half hour, he got the process of doing the right thing in motion.

SOLUTION #7 *Judge for Yourself*

The judge wants to know if he should violate the rules of court procedure to prevent likely harm to the community. His question is, "What is more important, the rules of the court or the good of the community?" The judge thinks that the *global benefit approach* is directing him to ignore court procedure and allow the prisoner to be found guilty "for the good of the community." Since the *global benefit approach* cannot give an answer by itself, we can see what is wrong with this line of reasoning. If the judge allows the prisoner to be found guilty, he violates a ground rule he is sworn to uphold, which is that judges should uphold the law regardless of their personal opinions. This ground rule itself provides great benefit to the community. The judge is too focused on the potential short-term harm caused by the prisoner to consider the broader harm of having judges violate court procedure as they see fit.

SOLUTION #8 *Dead River*

The problem in the Dead River case is that holding the companies accountable today for what they did in the distant past punishes current managers, employees, and shareholders for deeds in which they had no part. On the other hand, if the companies are not held accountable, the people who live along the river will be punished for something they did not do and companies will be able to escape responsibility for their actions merely by outliving them. This dispute went to trial with the sides taking the above stances. A mistrial was declared. It became evident to the parties to this dispute that settling matters in court would serve no one's purpose. The parties themselves had to reach agreement, which, to the surprise of many, they did. Because the competing ground rules of the two sides could not be brought into agreement, the two sides took the process to the next step, which is to look at the interests involved. The companies agreed to pay those who lived along the river a significant amount. Even though there was no agreement on ground rules, it was possible to achieve agreement based on interests.

SOLUTION #9 *Private Interests*

Changing accounting practices in midstream is clearly intended to deceive the company's investors and regulators, not to mention its resellers, vendors, and other business partners. If there were no intention to deceive, the change in accounting practices could be openly announced. Of course, were it openly announced it would serve no purpose, since everyone would see the company's dire financial circumstances. On the other hand, if the move succeeds and the company goes on to prosper, this deceit will get little attention.

When I looked at this situation with the CEO, I encouraged him to believe that he could pull the company through while being candid about his actions. The CEO decided to be up front about the change in accounting practices while pointing out that many other high-tech firms already used this approach. While the next generation of products was not very successful, the CEO kept the company going on the strength of his reputation for leading struggling companies in the past.

SOLUTION #10   *Easy Conscience*

Our terminal patient refuses, for religious reasons, to allow the plug (on further therapeutic treatment) to be pulled , but on the other hand requests that everything be done to reduce his pain to the maximum extent possible. I do not think you can permit administration of a level of painkillers sure to result in death, unless the patient fully understands and consents to what is happening. The patient is asking his caregivers to accept responsibility for his death, while avoiding this responsibility himself. There are many permutations and coloring facts in any situation such as this one. If I were in the patient's shoes, I would want to take responsibility for what happens to me. Indeed, I could not put my family and caregivers in a situation in which they may doubt whether or not they are murderers.

SOLUTION #11   *Heart of Africa*

The CEO went to visit the company's South African employees, who numbered in the thousands, and the company town in which many of them lived. He wanted to *stand in their shoes*. The company's emissaries to the country's anti-apartheid groups came back with surprising news. The response was that they did not want to see more of their constituents thrust into poverty. They suggested that the company remain in South Africa, publicly explain its reasons for staying despite its objections to apartheid, and work with the anti-apartheid groups to end apartheid. The CEO was deeply moved by the appeals of the company's South African employees, and contrary to his closest peers, allowed the company to operate in South Africa to see the end of apartheid. Many of his company's South African employees and their children played a key role in the first post-apartheid governments. The CEO of this company not only stayed in South Africa, but also took many actions to ensure the end of apartheid.

My Ethical Workplace
An Organizational Assessment Tool

Throughout *Make an Ethical Difference,* we emphasized that ethics is not just about seeing what is right. Seeing what is right should lead naturally to doing what is right. While there are many places where you can be a source of ethical influence, your own workplace is a good place to start.

In order to help you assess your workplace, we have developed a tool called *My Ethical Workplace* to measure its strengths and weaknesses. This tool is based on research conducted over the past 25 years.

Once you know the strengths and weaknesses of your workplace, you will have a good idea where to apply our tools for making an ethical difference. Because you will be allowed to use *My Ethical Workplace* up to five times in a twelve-month period, you can also measure your progress.

You may also print your results, forward them to others, and ask others to use the tool to create a more complete picture of your workplace. You can even arrange to have departments or whole organizations use *My Ethical Workplace.* The more people who use the tool, the better your chances of succeeding as a source of ethical influence.

This unique online product is available at

http://www.bkconnection.com/my-ethical-workplace-oa.

Notes

1. The term *stakeholder* can be used responsibly. For example, see Freeman, Harrison, and Wicks, *Managing for Stakeholders: Survival, Reputation and Success* (New Haven: Yale University Press, 2007).

2. Adam Smith, *Theory of the Moral Sentiments,* 1759.

3. Stanley Milgram, "Behavioral Study of Obedience," *Journal of Abnormal and Social Psychology* 67 (1963): 371–78.

4. Philip G. Zimbardo et al, "A Pirandellian Prison," *The New York Times Magazine* (April 8, 1973): 38–45.

5. Stanley Milgram, *Obedience to Authority* (New York: Harper and Row, 1974): 37–8.

6. *The Compact Edition of the Oxford English Dictionary* (Oxford: Oxford University Press, 1971): 3955.

7. *The Compact Edition of the Oxford English Dictionary* (Oxford: Oxford University Press, 1971): 3207.

8. Thomas J. Peters and Robert H. Waterman, Jr., *In Search of Excellence* (New York: Harper and Row, 1982). Many academics have repudiated Peters and Waterman's approach but their approach is still influential in business.

9. See the interview of Rebecca Saxe by Gareth Cook, "The Mind Theorist," *Scientific American,* 307 no. 6 (December 2012): 74–7 and additional references included therein. See also Michael Gazzaniga's *The Ethical Brain: The Science of Our Moral Dilemmas* (New York: Dana Press, 2005).

10. New York: Random House, 1997.

11. "Ethics and Foreign Corrupt Practices Act," *Business Horizons* (December 1980): 43–7.

12. The Organisation For Economic Co-operation and Development (OECD) launched a largely ineffective anti-bribery campaign in the middle 1990s and the United Kingdom passed the far more effective Bribery Act 2010 in 2010.

13. There is also a form of Medicare called Choice or Part C that falls under the managed care model.

Index

197

About the Author

Mark Pastin walked away from a full, tenured professorship. When Mark left academia, he was serving as founding Director of the Lincoln Center for Ethics and Professor of Management at the W. P. Carey School of Business at Arizona State University. He is the author of over 100 academic and trade publications.

Mark left academia to prove that it is possible to create lasting ethical change in organizations. While Mark was transitioning from academia to his current work, he worked as a newspaper columnist, investment banker, and international consultant. Since 1993, Mark has served as Chief Executive Officer of the Council of Ethical Organizations, a nonprofit organization dedicated to promoting ethics in business, government, and the professions.

Throughout these careers, Mark has pursued practical approaches to ethical issues. His research focuses on two topics. The first topic is how to gain ethical insight and the second is how to translate that insight into ethical action.

When working toward his Ph.D. at Harvard University, Mark studied under two of the leading ethicists of the past hundred years, Roderick Firth and John Rawls. His studies focused on the unique human attributes that allow individuals to gain insight into ethical issues.

Mark realized that you could not claim ethical insight if this insight did not translate into ethical action. Simply put, the only relevant laboratory for ethical knowledge is the world in which we live and work. It is this insight that drove Mark to build a global consultancy in the area of organizational ethics.

This consultancy has spanned five continents, over thirty Fortune 500 companies, numerous smaller companies, domestic and international federal governments, and two presidential campaigns. He has advised corporations and governments in the United States, Brazil, Switzerland, Canada, Japan, Hong Kong, the United Kingdom, Germany, Korea, Belgium, Australia, France, and Taiwan. His clients have included such corporations as American Express, Motorola, Medtronic, National Medical Enterprises, Intel, GE, NYNEX, Caterpillar, Oxford Health, MCI, Lincoln Electric, GTECH, Texas Instruments, GlaxoSmithKline, the Williams Companies, National Health Laboratories, Pinnacle West Capital Corporation, Cadbury Schweppes, John Deere, and many others. His ethics work brought him considerable acclaim in Japan, where he spoke to a single audience of 10,000.

Mark's work and publications have been featured in such publications as *The Wall Street Journal, Forbes,* the *International Herald Tribune, The New York Times,* and *BusinessWeek.* He has received support from the National Science Foundation, the National Endowment for the Humanities, the Earhart Foundation, the Exxon Foundation, and other sources.

Through his work, Mark has developed tools to help organizations gain and act on ethical insight. These tools bring about ethical improvement by enhancing the overall performance of an organization. *Make an Ethical Difference* brings together cases of ethical improvement drawn from actual experience, tools for making and acting on ethical decisions, and practical lessons usable by individuals and organizations of all types and sizes.

Mark is based in Alexandria, Virginia, where he lives with his wife, Christina, and five bossy French bulldogs.

Working with the Author

Mark Pastin works with organizations and individuals to address complex ethical and compliance issues. Mark and his team of experienced ethics and compliance professionals help organizations meet the day-to-day challenges involved in leading an ethical organization. Consulting activities may include creating codes of conduct, providing education and training programs, writing policies and procedures, and issues management. Mark is also often called upon to conduct assessments of an organization's ethics or compliance program. Mark has worked with the Council of Ethical Organizations and other organizations to build a database of best practices in ethics and compliance. He is the author of the Ethics-Compliance Survey, a validated survey instrument for assessing the ethics and compliance environment of organizations. This instrument is not only widely used by companies worldwide, it also has been used by some of the largest federal agencies in the United States.

Mark has spoken to hundreds of national and international organizations, including many colleges and universities, domestically and internationally. Each of his presentations is tailored to the group he is addressing. Mark's presentations emphasize interaction with the audience and receive uniformly high reviews. He not only speaks on corporate and international ethics, he is also a frequent presenter on medical and healthcare ethics.

In addition to his speaking engagements, Mark has created a number of courses for individuals and organizations that want to learn to apply the tools in *Make an Ethical Difference*. His best known course is the Ethics-Quality Equation, which teaches participants how to build ethics and quality into everything they do. You can reach Mark at councile@aol.com and read Mark's blog at http://ethicswhisperer.com.

Berrett–Koehler
Publishers

A community dedicated to creating
a world that works for all

Dear Reader,

Thank you for picking up this book and joining our worldwide community of Berrett-Koehler readers. We share ideas that bring positive change into people's lives, organizations, and society.

To welcome you, we'd like to offer you a free e-book. You can pick from among twelve of our bestselling books by entering the promotional code **BKP92E** here: http://www.bkconnection.com/welcome.

When you claim your free e-book, we'll also send you a copy of our e-newsletter, the *BK Communiqué*. Although you're free to unsubscribe, there are many benefits to sticking around. In every issue of our newsletter you'll find

- A free e-book
- Tips from famous authors
- Discounts on spotlight titles
- Hilarious insider publishing news
- A chance to win a prize for answering a riddle

Best of all, our readers tell us, "Your newsletter is the only one I actually read." So claim your gift today, and please stay in touch!

Sincerely,

Charlotte Ashlock
Steward of the BK Website

Questions? Comments? Contact me at bkcommunity@bkpub.com.